GRIEF
DEMYSTIFIED

GRIEF

DEMYSTIFIED

AN INTRODUCTION

CAROLINE LLOYD

Jessica Kingsley *Publishers*
London and Philadelphia

On page 6, the poem 'Resilience' by Christina Thatcher, copyright © 2017 Christina Thatcher, is reprinted with kind permission of Christina Thatcher. On page 84, the monoprint 'The Usher' by Alysia Trackim, copyright © 2017 Alysia Trackim, is reproduced with kind permission of Alysia Trackim.

Figures 3.2 and 5.1 kindly provided by Rustam Eltman.

First published in 2018
by Jessica Kingsley Publishers
73 Collier Street
London N1 9BE, UK
and
400 Market Street, Suite 400
Philadelphia, PA 19106, USA

www.jkp.com

Library of Congress Cataloging in Publication Data
A CIP catalog record for this book is available from the Library of Congress

British Library Cataloguing in Publication Data
A CIP catalogue record for this book is available from the British Library

ISBN 978 1 78592 313 5
eISBN 978 1 78450 624 7

Printed and bound in the United States

In memory of Charlie

RESILIENCE

Shuddering I walk past it,
the dead pigeon on my way to work
always in the same position
but each day with fewer feathers,
less organs, more leaves.

Even though it upsets me
and there are more pleasant ways
to go – I still choose this path,
still slow down and look directly
at the bird's soft, open body,

force myself to internalize the loss,
hoping that one day
I'll accept it.

Christina Thatcher

CONTENTS

FOREWORD

It's 12:15pm on Wednesday 24 May 2017, and I'm at Leeds City Museum listening to a talk by Caroline Lloyd about grief, demystified. Caroline has PowerPoint slides and she does refer to them now and again; however, there is a marker pen in her hand which she uses more frequently and animatedly to draw diagrams on the flip-chart paper beside her. She commentates as she draws, excitement pushing the pen faster and, at points, making grooves in the page. Caroline's passion for her subject is palpable.

It is contagious too, and I find myself nodding along, making notes and then underlining certain words in the hope that a future me will be able to re-connect with what I am experiencing here in this lecture room. Caroline starts talking about hierarchies of grief and I'm inching closer and closer to the edge of my seat. It's exciting for me because experiences of hierarchy, a sort of 'benchmarking', comparing and 'ranking' of grief, is something I'm observing in my own work. 'What theory is this?' I'm thinking. 'What book has Caroline taken this from? What paper can I read? … I must ask her afterwards.'

I did ask, and it turns out that Caroline hadn't read a book or paper on hierarchies of grief, but was presenting her own thinking (complete with diagram) born from her own experience. This phenomenon was something that, Caroline told me, she had observed as both a bereaved person and as a grief-support worker. For me as a researcher into death and bereavement, and as a psychologist who specialises in therapy, it resonated. As I have got to know Caroline and her work, this learning from experience is what I have observed to be at the centre of it – sensible, empathic and well-informed theories which speak to the heart of grief and bereavement.

Grief Demystified is described by Caroline as 'the book [she] wanted and needed when [she] was bereaved, and whilst she was training as a bereavement volunteer.' Initially however, Caroline set out writing for those working with grieving and bereaved individuals who are not what we might call at first glance 'counsellors'. *Grief Demystified* was designed for the police, funeral directors and nurses, so those individuals who work with the grieving and bereaved, yet who might have little training in the psychology of it all. The fundamental objective then, of *Grief Demystified*, was to present current thinking about grief and bereavement in an accessible way. Caroline has achieved this and, in doing so, has created so much more.

When Caroline first told me about *Grief Demystified*, I offered to review a chapter for her. I did so without realising that the initial intended audience was not practitioners like me. Thus, I began to read *Grief Demystified* through the lens of a therapy professional. I found it was everything that, as a practitioner, I wanted it to be. Our society is hugely influenced by the idea that grief comes at us in stages, each identifiable, each to be worked through, yet this was not what I was observing in my research or practice. The grief I saw in the therapy room did not come in such neat packages. Caroline's narrative was a relief to read. Here was theory which helped me to gain an informed sense of empathy. I had a background from which to understand grieving people, in language that was accessible to me, and which fitted genuinely with my own experiences and observations.

I volunteered to review the entire book and was struck by how useful *Grief Demystified* would have been for me, as an adjunct to therapy for particular clients. No person's difficulties come into the therapy room as a single entity. They are situated in a web of past and current experiences and difficulties, a strand of which, sometimes overlooked, is grief. I recall one such client, nearly ten years post-bereavement, seeking help for stress and anxiety. His initial understanding of the current problem was nothing to do with the death of a much-beloved parent. Yet, as we delved deeper, that seemed to be at the core of his pain. Floored by finding that his siblings had responded differently to the death, he would ask, 'Why is it me who is still affected?' 'Why do I cry at the slightest sign of stress?' If only I had the knowledge to say, 'Because it's the strength of the attachment which determines the level of grief, not the label.' Underneath, this client was really telling me that they believed they were not normal. As a result, they had looked for reasons why they were 'different' and had decided that it was because there was something 'wrong' with them, some weakness, some lack of character. If only I had had *Grief Demystified* then to help normalise and validate his experience. Sometimes a book, which has been well-structured and which can be digested at the reader's own pace, can be more powerful than an attempt to explain verbally to a client what it is that you want them to know. Sometimes a book can, no pun intended, help to get you and your client on the same page.

So I'd established that *Grief Demystified* was a gift to non-therapy practitioners, and I'd established that it was a gift also to therapists, but there was something else too. I had a felt-sense that this knowledge, presented as it was, would be useful for the grieving masses also. Caroline's narrative is so embedded in experience, so 'on point' with the nuances of bereavement, that its potential to normalise grief and grief behaviours felt too important to miss. I tested this theory by giving her manuscript to a dear friend to read. Charlotte is in her 80s and is mourning the loss of her husband, the love of her life, who died in the spring of 2016. When I asked for her honest opinion on the book, Charlotte (who read it in less than two days) told me that it had been a benefit to her. She explained that it 'brings home' to her what grief is, and I've not heard her say 'I should be getting over this' to me since.

How many grieving people are affected by this idea that we need to work through 'stages' and 'get over' our bereavement? How many 'benchmark' their process against the common discourses and conclude, despairingly, that they are not 'doing it properly'? It's not easy to be a griever or a grief worker in a society where the dominant discourse is not one which normalises or even talks about grief and grief behaviours. Often, in the West, we struggle to talk about death. More common bereavements carry enough difficulty, enough awkwardness, and when it comes to suicides, murders, the death of children, often disenfranchised deaths like miscarriages and pet death, we are at even more of a loss for words. *Grief Demystified* provides a narrative for us to understand and communicate about all types of death. It teaches us about what grief looks like, not just what we expect to see but what really occurs in the quiet moments, when no one is looking. *Grief Demystified* gives practical advice, questions to ask and phrases to use to help us communicate with grievers and support them to share their story. We are given contact details for organisations from which to seek further advice. The chapters of *Grief Demystified* consider if and when grief becomes problematic from a mental health perspective. Caroline tells us about the importance of wider networks and urges us to take care of grievers from a systemic perspective, weaving a net of support which can catch them if they fall. She also urges practitioners to take care of themselves with a section on compassion fatigue which I found to be illuminating, normalising and validating.

For all grief workers – practitioners, volunteers, friends and family – Caroline's narrative is a light to guide us through what can be the dark and confusing landscape of grief.

Dr Jennifer Dayes, Counselling Psychologist

ACKNOWLEDGEMENTS

This book was created to inform the bereaved, and further the education of those who are supporting grievers. What you are reading is a team effort; beginning with the researchers who tirelessly work to improve our knowledge, the volunteers and paid workers who support the bereaved and the grievers who inform our practice. This book could not have been written without any of them.

I'd like to acknowledge several instrumental contributors: Jon Crossley, my counselling mentor, for his unconditional support and modelling the true meaning of Roger's Core Conditions. Rosemary Hayes for the lightbulb moment and her endless patience. Professor Conor McGuckin and Dr Aoife M. Lynam for their unwavering faith and professional guidance, without whom this project would not have materialised, and I would not be the person I am evolving into. Their scholarly and pastoral advice, support and unrelenting guidance are hugely appreciated. To Dr Jennifer Dayes who gave her time and expertise so generously, her attention to detail and critical analysis have transformed this book entirely.

To my family, friends, colleagues and acquaintances who have been supportive I am deeply grateful.

INTRODUCTION

> You can't control the uncontrollable, and you
> can't make sense of the senseless.

Death is a natural part of the cycle of life. Grief is therefore the normal response to the loss of a loved one. According to the website of the Global Ecology Network, there are an estimated 55.3 million deaths per year globally; and whilst some cultures still acknowledge death, and grieve as their ancestors did, other cultures have become more avoidant.

As an independent subject, the study of bereavement is relatively new. It has been informed by many other disciplines, from religion, sociology, psychology, anthropology to the medical fields. From a layperson's perspective, very little theoretical knowledge has filtered through. There is one notable exception: the five stages of grief, which has been misinterpreted to great effect since its inception approximately 50 years ago (Kübler-Ross 1969).

With this lack of informed awareness, it is common to hear people say they are uncertain about how to talk about death, or how to communicate with the bereaved. This book seeks to provide evidence-based information and practical examples of how to address this.

Perceptions of grief can range from the belief that you should 'get over it', that you must cry a lot, and that if you don't feel a certain way within a prescribed amount of time you haven't grieved 'properly'. These are myths, and this book will explain their origins, and why they are inaccurate. It will also explore why grief varies with each person individually, and with each bereavement.

Evolution and changes within social environments in the Western world have also compounded the myths of grief. Historically, art and life were full of images of the reality of death, the dying and the *wretched* bereaved. The art produced in the Middle Ages is full of representations of the impact of the Black Death. Another example is the theme of death and the maiden, where women interact with representations of death. This can be traced back to ancient Greece, and is a common thread in classical art. However, representations of this type, and death itself, are viewed with a morbid curiosity or sometimes avoided in the 21st century. What was once visible and normal is now largely detached from daily life.

Philippe Ariès was a prominent scholar and novelist who wrote prolifically about the change in Western attitudes to death. He observed that before the 19th century, death was recognised and set aside in our societies, mourners were given space and time to grieve, and bereavement was accepted for the normal but life-changing event that it can be (Ariès 1991).

When Queen Victoria wore mourning clothes after Prince Albert died in 1861, the fashion for women was to demonstrate grief by wearing black clothing for periods that lasted up to two years. The use of stationery edged in black, the drawing of curtains, stopping clocks and children wearing black armbands were all common. These customs signalled to society that the family was bereaved, so they could be treated accordingly. Their grief was public and recognised. The Victorians also memorialised the deceased by taking photographs of them after death, either independently, or within family portraits. Another example was wearing jewellery that incorporated the dead person's hair. During this historical period these social rituals and signals normalised death and helped facilitate supported grieving.

An example of a Victorian family portrait, which commonly included the deceased

In the 19th century there were death-themed nightclubs in Paris, where the living engaged with representations of the dead. The following is a description of these environments:

Large, heavy, wooden coffins, resting on biers, were ranged about the room in an order suggesting the recent happening of a frightful catastrophe. The walls were decorated with skulls and bones, skeletons in grotesque attitudes, battle-pictures, and guillotines in action. (Morrow and Cucuel 2013, p.265)

For the Victorians, *death was seen, dying was normal and grief was expected.* Yet public mourning fell out of fashion in the Edwardian era, and this was followed by religious changes and medical improvements. The high rate of death in the two world wars also had a transformational effect that led to death and grief slowly disappearing from public view.

It could be argued that the First World War was a catalyst to this detachment, due to the overwhelming numbers of deaths, particularly of young men. The sheer scale of the bereaved population led to active measures being taken by the government to discourage public mourning (Brennen and Hardt 1999). They had to ensure the public remained engaged with the political climate, so cinema and newspaper messaging was constructed with positivity, and dwelling on the deaths and casualties of war was discouraged. Governments needed to ensure that people did not become uncontrollable, despondent and unresponsive to the war effort. Focus was centred on the greater good of society, and not to become 'self-indulgent' with grief. There were so many war casualties that virtually everyone was in mourning, and whilst this was still reflected with black or subdued clothing, the customary length of time was shortened to a few months.

Whilst this left Western societies with a culture of resilience, it also left a legacy of reduced public significance and support for the bereaved. It was something to 'get on with' and 'get over'. Death had gradually evolved into a subject that was rarely discussed, and grief became a private affair; curtains were no longer drawn, clocks were no longer stopped, the public displays of mourning were no longer observed (Petch n.d.).

Improved medical care has further separated the public from death. Where once death was largely due to infectious diseases such as plague, degenerative diseases have replaced them as the main cause of death. There are increased expectations of longevity, continual advances in treatments, and dying is largely medicalised within hospices and hospitals.

Death and dying were historically incorporated within the home, and it was common for families to witness these processes. Families also attended to the bodies, and natural decomposition was witnessed. Funeral directors have replaced families in carrying out these functions, and commonly take the bodies directly from the place of death to their premises until the funeral. These shifts from within the family and home to external services, coupled with the expectation that medical conditions can be treated and/or cured, has further led to the perception of a 'death-denying society'. However, this 'denial of death' can vary between individuals and communities and often depends on factors such as personal experience and cultural background. For many, death has become, or is, a taboo subject. However, it could be said that the concerns being raised by academics and professionals working within the death, dying and bereavement fields, around this post-war medicalisation, and the professionalisation of death, are leading to a shift in death consciousness. The hospice movement, palliative care concerns, Dignitas, online memorialisation sites, social media, pre-paid funeral plan advertising, bereavement support charities, the evolution of the study of death and bereavement (thanatology) as an academic discipline, internet resources, social media and blogs all contribute to open discussion and dialogue around death, dying and bereavement.

Specific events have also addressed these topics. One example is Life.Death.Whatever, a festival first held in London in 2016 with death-related art installations, bereavement workshops, eclectic talks, death-themed cocktails and hand-written memorial notes. There were also coffins that adults and children wrote on and sat in, filled with brightly coloured plastic balls that were played with.

Another example is the death café movement. The concept originated with the sociologist Bernard Crettaz, who held the first *café mortel* in 2004 in Switzerland. This has evolved into the death café model, created by the late Jon Underwood, a self-described 'death entrepreneur'. Death cafés are self-directed discussions where members of the public gather to discuss the topics of death and life. The model has been increasing in popularity throughout the world since 2010.

Events such as Life.Death.Whatever and the death café movement represent a rejection of our avoidance of the subject of death.

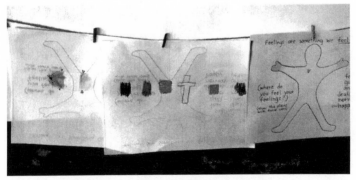

Artwork from a facilitated children's grief workshop in London during Life.Death.Whatever in 2016

The internet has also created a new forum for death conversations and public grieving. Are we witnessing a rejection of a death-denying culture, and the creation of a modern grieving era?

Where once the hair of the deceased was incorporated into jewellery, now the ashes of the dead are incorporated into fireworks, tattoos, diamonds, vinyl records, hourglasses, teddy bears, portraits, pencils, stained glass, trees and even bongs!

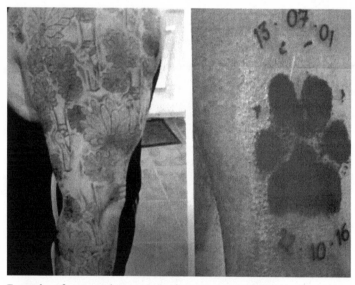

Examples of memorial tattoos: the first incorporates the deceased wife's ashes into a story of her life as a professional dancer; the second is a memorial to their beloved dog

Despite these evolutionary changes, some people still find these subjects difficult to discuss. The phrases 'passed away', 'passed on', 'slipped away', 'gone', 'lost', 'deceased', 'kicked the bucket', 'pushing up daisies' and 'fell asleep in Jesus' are interwoven in obituaries, tombstones and the media to somehow soften the blow and avoid the word 'dead'.

Death is certainty for all of us until, or if, in the future we can become immortal. But those interacting with the bereaved in their profession, or the bereaved searching for information, will know that modern research-based resources can be hard to find.

With this in mind, this book provides research-based information that is accessible to everyone. Each chapter in this book follows the same structure: an introduction and exploration of the topic, followed by practical exercises or examples. It will provide a basic understanding of modern bereavement theory and introduce the variables that contribute to why grief is unique for everyone.

Chapter 1

WHAT IS GRIEF?

Defining grief

Take a moment to think about how you would define grief.

Grief: The elephant in the room – examples
of definitions from grief workshops

As you can see in the picture, the perception and definition
of grief is different for everyone. A quick internet search

will show a myriad of definitions and a variety of metaphors. This is largely due to individual interpretation and the different perspectives from differing disciplines. For simplicity, in this book, the following definition will be used:

> Bereavement is the loss experienced by an individual of a valued relationship.

Grief could be considered the feelings, thoughts and actions we experience after the death of a significant attachment, and the re-organisation and adjustment of our world without that person in it. When a loss occurs, there is an adjustment and adaptation to the new circumstances, and this process is called grieving. The word 'grief' may refer to other losses, but death is different: it is finite, the end of a life, and for this reason other losses are excluded from this book.

The way someone reacts, feels and responds, the actions they take, the inactions they choose all depend on the nature of the relationship with the deceased. *Normal* grief involves acceptance of the death and subsequent losses, and the building of a new world around it in a gradual way. Grief can feel like a disconnection from 'real' life.

In time, the acute feelings will diminish. This can take many years in some cases, but it is a progressive and normal process. However, there can be deviations, which will be explored in Chapter 4.

Grief has emotional, cognitive, spiritual, physical and behavioural manifestations that can be completely overwhelming and debilitating. Everyone is unique, and each relationship built and maintained with others is unique, so the feelings that follow a bereavement will be equally unique.

However, there are common feelings that follow a death, which can include: sadness, shock, anxiety, loneliness, guilt, anger, depression, lethargy, yearning, abandonment, helplessness, fear, upset and confusion. People may feel all, some or none of those feelings, but what is certain is that there is ordinarily a sense of loss – loss of the loved one, loss of the roles they played in their life, loss of an imagined future, and the loss of their identity in relation to the deceased. For example, if a man's wife dies, have they lost their identity as a 'husband'? Are they now a 'widower'?

There has also been an expansion from the traditional view that grief was wholly emotional, to one that recognises all the other issues that need to be considered, which can include:

- *Health changes*: Research has shown that the bereaved are more susceptible to physical and psychological ailments and illnesses, including heart problems, anxiety and depression (APA 2013; Carey *et al.* 2014).

- *Cognitive changes*: The bereaved often talk about the 'fog' of grief, of being confused and having impaired thinking processes, including forgetfulness and absent-mindedness. A loss of confidence can be a big issue for some people to deal with, particularly after the death of a best friend or spouse/partner. Cognitive responses can also range from wondering why their loved one died, to asking how they are going to cope.

- *Social changes*: These are varied and depend on individual circumstances but can include losing friends and being treated differently. Changes can also involve joining clubs and support groups after bereavement.

- *Cultural aspects*: The mix of values, beliefs, traditions and rituals that a cultural group share will influence their expression of grief.

- *Spiritual dimensions*: Grief can shatter the assumptive world, and a common response to a death, particularly of a child, is changed opinion on previously held spiritual beliefs. Death can also lead to a strengthened commitment to an existing belief.

- *Behavioural manifestations*: Behaviour can change whilst the bereaved are grieving or once they have adjusted to life after the death. These can include changes in dietary patterns, the desire to smoke or drink more, as well as sleep anomalies. Where once the bereaved used to enjoy particular activities, they may detach from them, or they may find enjoyment in new activities.

These are all examples and are not exhaustive. To state the obvious, grief is the cost of loving someone: the greater the love, the greater the loss, the greater the impact.

The more entwined two people are with each other emotionally and/or physically, the more significant their absence will be to the one who is left behind. When someone significant dies, grief is all-encompassing, but it is normal for people of the same family to have different grief experiences, because their relationship with the deceased was different.

Relationships can also have difficulties, and this should be recognised. If the death occurs at a time of conflicting emotions, grief can be affected by guilt or resentment, sometimes even anger or any other response. That does not detract from the significance of the loss, but it can complicate the emotional reactions.

Grief isn't prescriptive; it doesn't have a timeline or a set pattern. There is no benchmarking to see if someone's grieving is 'poor', 'average', 'good' or 'excellent' against a prescribed formula or table. Sadly, the five stages of grief model by Elisabeth Kübler-Ross has been misinterpreted in this way. Elisabeth herself said that they were never meant to imply that emotions can be tucked into neat packages, and she emphasised that there is no typical response to loss.

Attachment and proximity

The impact of a death can vary considerably and is dependent on the nature of the relationship and what has been lost. The proximity of the relationship is an important element and can be physical and/or emotional. One example of proximity in a joint physical and emotional way is when spouses are bereaved. When two people are emotionally attached and live together, the losses are significant and can be overwhelming, particularly if the surviving spouse was reliant on the deceased. When someone is absent after being present every day, there is a huge gap in routine and support.

This can also apply to any relationship that is physically close, such as neighbours, friends and co-workers, whether this involves living together or being in regular contact. The more someone is involved in a life, the greater their presence will be missed. The depth of loss in such relationships can sometimes be overlooked because they may not be recognised as significant.

The internet and smartphones have changed the concept of proximity. Skype, Facetime and other programmes and applications allow people to be connected through a virtual medium. Connecting with someone regularly via technology is sufficient to create the same bonds as physical presence, and the grief resulting from the loss of these relationships should be acknowledged.

Emotional proximity is explained through attachment theory, with attachment defined as 'a deep and enduring emotional bond that connects one person to another across time and space' (Ainsworth 1973; Bowlby 1969). To use a metaphor: attachments can be compared to the roots of trees and when that tree is forcibly removed from the ground – the deeper the roots, the bigger the hole that is left.

Attachment theory is a model that explains what is referred to as the attachment style of individuals. Each person's style is thought to represent the way a person attaches to others and, subsequently, reacts to loss. The theory arose in infant studies and has since expanded to studies of adult couples (Hazan and Shaver 1987). There are three major types of attachments: *secure* (where a person feels safe and secure in a relationship), *avoidant* (where a person is independent and may not seek help) and *insecure* (where a person tends towards being clingy and may find it difficult to adjust to the death). These are simplified summaries of the theory, which is explained in more detail in Chapter 3. The fourth attachment style is 'disorganised attachment', which is beyond the scope of this book.

Attachment style can be an indicator of the type of relationship between two people and of how that person will express their grief. Those who form secure attachments should have sufficient support from other securely attached relationships; conversely, those who are more insecure may be overly dependent on others for support; while those who are more avoidant may not demonstrate the significance of their loss.

One of the myths explored in Chapter 2 is that the label of the relationship determines the loss. It is not that simple: it is the attachment that determines the nature and depth of the loss, not the label.

For example, some people have deeper attachments to a step-parent than to a parent, but the perception of society is that we grieve more deeply for a parent than a step-parent. First-person narrative stories in the media generally perpetuate these generalisations of 'traditional' familial relationships with two parents and siblings. Many families are extended, with step-parents, same-sex couples and other non-traditional structures. Bonds are also significant for people who are not close to their family (either physically or emotionally) and have created a 'family' of friends. Step-families, fostered children, work colleagues and friends are all examples of significant attachments that transcend the traditional family structure. Therefore, care should be taken to ascertain the nature of the attachment before assuming an understanding of the loss.

Attachment also extends to pets, which are considered by some to be integral to their life and emotional wellbeing, and the death of a beloved pet can have the same impact as the loss of a human relationship.

Grief and death

Traditional academic views of grief and bereavement have been replaced by a new understanding born out of research conducted over the past 30 years. However, very little of this has filtered through to society in general, and outdated information continues to circulate.

The notion that grief has a predetermined trajectory, starting with emotional distress, following predictable stages, and ending with 'recovery' or the expectation of 'getting over it', is not supported by research. The idea that grief 'work' (i.e. the act of *doing* something, for example progressing through stages or other indicators) is necessary to 'recovery' is outdated, and unhelpfully positions grief, as an illness. We are now aware of the healthy role of maintaining continued bonds with the deceased, and this should be encouraged. The deceased are no longer physically present, but they live on in history, biology and memory. Their legacy will always remain in one form or another, and it is healthy to recognise and celebrate this fact. 'Recovery' suggests the deceased are left behind and the bereaved have 'moved on': that they were somewhat ill and needed intervention to recover. Chapter 2 will explore this further.

Grief, however, can be a trigger for someone who is vulnerable to anxiety or depression. Dr Michael Miller, editor of the *Harvard Mental Health Letter* and assistant professor of psychiatry at Harvard Medical School is quoted as saying, 'for some people who have previously struggled with acknowledged or unacknowledged depression, the death of a significant other can be the catalyst that brings depression to the foreground' (Nowinski 2012).

For those who may be predisposed to medical conditions, support can mitigate further occurrences. Ideally, this is provided by family and friends but can also be provided within a suitable therapeutic setting (i.e. a place where the bereaved are allowed to experience all the feelings, thoughts and actions that accompany grief). The bereaved may need to share stories, memories and emotions, and, as these are perfectly natural human responses, they should be encouraged. Not acknowledging the deceased either by name or reference can be extremely upsetting, they may feel that their loved one has been erased from history.

Grieving for public figures

Reacting in an emotional way to the death of someone famous may seem odd to some because there may be a lack of understanding surrounding the relationship. It is quite common for fans to grieve the death of their idol. Even though many people do not have a close personal relationship with the deceased, they may have followed them and their progress for a large part of their life. Interviews provide personal details, revealing more than their public persona may display, and these allow fans to form attachments. The media and internet bring famous people into proximity with their fans. They can be seen, heard, and read about for 24 hours a day, seven days a week.

This ever-increasing accessibility (e.g. via social media and personal websites) allows the formation of connections to the famous, who are admired, respected or adored.

These intimate, personal communications can have a great impact on individuals. For example, many teenagers retreat into a world of music or other hobbies and form attachments with their idols. As they learn to adjust to life from childhood to adulthood, with all the difficulties that may ensue, these connections can be intense and long-lasting. It seems rational that when their idol dies, a sense of loss therefore occurs.

A history of grief theory

The origins of grief theory stem from the pastoral care offered in religion and our study of biology, such as Charles Darwin's observation of emotion in animals. This evolved within the psychological arena when Freud produced his paper *Mourning and Melancholia* in 1917, during World War One. This context, as mentioned previously, was within an environment of overwhelming deaths. The central tenet of Freud's theory on grief was that there had to be a complete emotional detachment from the deceased so that emotional energy could be reinvested into someone or something else. He believed that emotional reserves are finite. This is where the notion of 'getting over' the death of someone originates. It was an individual perspective where the bereaved were expected to retract, detach and then reintegrate within relationships.

Freud wrote that the bereaved needed to be freed from the deceased, that there had to be a readjustment to life without the deceased, and that new relationships could be built unencumbered so that they could go back to being 'normal' as quickly as possible. His view was that any deviation from this process needed *intervention*, because they were at increased risk of physical and mental illness. This framework is still evident within societal expectations today, despite many theories and research papers contradicting this approach. It is still common to hear that someone hasn't grieved 'properly', with the misconception that this means complete detachment or 'getting over' the death. Freud was himself significantly bereaved several times, including the death of his daughter and beloved grandson. In his private letters, he spoke of the impact of these bereavements for many years after their deaths, but it is unclear whether he felt he had untreated complicated grief or whether he espoused one thing but experienced another. We can conclude that his professional promotion of complete detachment appears to be at odds with his personal experiences of bereavement.

Another lingering myth can be traced back to a paper written by psychoanalyst Helene Deutsch in 1937 (see Roazen 1992), which stated that outward grieving is essential to complete the grieving process. This contributed to the idea that you *must* express your emotions outwardly to be considered 'normal'. Even as recently as the 1980s Vamik Volkan, a psychiatrist and author, believed that anyone 'resisting mourning' should be challenged by their counsellor, and that this was key to successful treatment (Volkan 1981). Modern academic literature completely debunks the misconception that everyone should grieve in the same way for every bereavement. Grieving styles will be explored in more detail later in the book.

Whilst Freud's work was pioneering, and provided a structure and platform on which to build, later theorists overlaid his approach with staged models, beginning with psychiatrist Erich Lindemann in 1944. He studied

101 people who were bereaved, and formulated four chronological stages: shock, sadness and withdrawal, anger, and then return to normal. This was very early research and was formulated on a small sample of his patients, but it was the start of the evolution of bereavement as a distinct academic area.

The most notorious and oft-quoted staged model is that of Elisabeth Kübler-Ross, developed in the 1960s. Her five-stage model was constructed from research based on patients who had been diagnosed with terminal illness within a hospice environment. She expanded the model to include bereavement and other losses in later years, but was explicit that the stages were not intended to be interpreted as linear.

Earlier and later stage theorists, who produced models based specifically on grief following a bereavement, seem to be overlooked. Grief counsellor and therapist J. William Worden, psychiatrist Colin Murray Parkes, who built upon Bowlby's work, and clinical psychologist Therese Rando are examples of academics and grief experts that are not as well known outside of the realms of academia.

Worden, for example, has furthered the knowledge of phases of grief and evolved his theories in line with updated research. His view of bereavement involves adapting to loss and states his four tasks *may* be involved in mourning (Worden 2010, p.39). The tasks are:

- *Task I: To Accept the Reality of the Loss.* No one wants to be separated permanently from someone they love, so accepting that they will never see them again or have them physically in their life is a difficult adjustment. Denial of the loss and not talking about the debilitating nature of the permanence of death can be more painful for grievers than the actual grief itself. Acknowledgement and acceptance are critical to *normal* grief.

- *Task II: To Process the Pain of Grief.* The physical and emotional pain of grief will vary depending on the person and the nature of the loss. Sometimes, as a society, it is easier for onlookers to avoid the bereaved or encourage them to engage in distracting activities rather than allow them to speak about their feelings, talk about the bereaved or simply take time out. This can be especially true when someone is obligated to return to work quickly following a significant bereavement. Grief can be a slow process to endure and the fast pace of current Western life can sometimes hinder what is natural.

- *Task III: To Adjust to a World without the Deceased.* Finding a new 'normal' is difficult and there can be many adjustments to be made. Secondary losses, such as identity, status, friends and financial loss can make it even harder, but adjustment is unavoidable. Life continues without the deceased, and there is a period of learning to reconcile the loss of the roles played by the loved one in their life, and learning how to tackle those roles themselves.

- *Task IV: To Find an Enduring Connection with the Deceased in the Midst of Embarking on a New Life.* This can be a difficult phase for the bereaved, particularly bereaved parents who feel that 'moving on' is leaving their child 'behind' and is disloyal.

> Continuing a relationship with the deceased is finding a way to incorporate them within their 'new' life, whilst still acknowledging their importance and keeping a connection to their 'old' life.

Stage models are often used as a reference point for grief in articles in the popular press. However, their authors are often quoting them without fully appreciating their context or message. The academics who formulated and published staged/phased models based on bereavement research have specific contextual messages. They state that grief is not linear. Grievers weave in and out of phases, but not all grievers experience all the areas identified within the models. These stage-based models were not intended to be used as prescriptive exercises.

Although there may be commonalities when observing grief, the identified stages in stage-based models do not apply to all people, all the time. Therein lies the problem; grief is the result of many variables related to the bereavement, and any further losses (secondary losses) because of the death are therefore just as variable. These models remain popular because they appeal to those who would like to impose structure on what can be an overwhelming emotional rollercoaster. They can also allow a bereaved person, and those supporting them, to feel as though they are in control, as if they can track their 'progress' through a series of predictable stages. The reality of grief is that it can be unpredictable and uncontrollable.

Despite their popularity, stage models are often criticised for neglecting grief reactions other than the emotional (Kilcrease 2008; Shermer 2008). They can be used to oversimplify what is usually a complex range of responses, and ignore other impactful factors such as the social or the physical.

Modern research-based theory

Research has progressed significantly from Freud's professional opinion in 1917 that it was necessary for the bereaved to undertake complete emotional detachment from the deceased loved one in order to 'reattach' to someone else. Modern research contradicts Freud's original theory. For example, Klass, Silverman and Nickman (1996) reported that maintaining emotional bonds with a loved one (continuing bonds) is healthy. Those who have been bereaved will recognise that although their loved one has died, the attachment (love) remains in a variety of different ways, depending on the relationship. Ironically, this resonates with the fact that Freud talked about the lasting impact of his grief 30 years after his daughter's death.

Continuing bonds can be expressed in many ways: emotionally, cognitively, spiritually and physically. These can be either private or publicly shared. One example is the relocation of the deceased to 'heaven', and the imagining of a continuous 'life' there. Other private ways can be talking to the deceased, or memorialising them through rituals. For example, this can be as simple as placing certain flowers on the grave on a particular day. Public examples are gravestones, visiting the grave, scattering ashes, planting trees, online memorial sites, memorial photo albums and so on. Virtually everything that includes the deceased after they have died is a continuing bond and is a healthy and normal part of grieving.

One interesting example of continuing bonds is the 'wind phone' in Japan. Itsaru Sasaki installed a phone booth in his garden in 2011, a year before the tsunami and earthquake devastated the region, to cope with the death of his cousin. He wanted the conversations with his deceased cousin to be 'carried on the wind'. Following the deaths of almost 16,000 in the disaster, the public have been using the 'wind phone' and it is estimated that over 10,000 people have visited it.

The notion that grief has an ending or that you 'get over it' has therefore been rejected and a continuing relationship is to be embraced. Worden referred to this in his phased model as 'Task IV: To Find an Enduring Connection with the Deceased in the Midst of Embarking on a New Life'. His earlier version in 1991 (prior to the publication of Klass *et al.*'s *Continuing Bonds: New Understandings of Grief* in 1996) was 'to find a place for the deceased that will enable the mourner to be connected with the deceased but in a way that will not preclude him or her from going on with life' (p.50).

As outlined above, until the 1990s stage or phase models and the notion of a 'completion' of grief prevailed, and this helps explain why newer research has yet to embed itself in wider society. Additionally, the targeted study and research of bereavement and grief, independent of other disciplines, is a relatively new academic field. The combination of these two factors, in the context of a general avoidance of the topics of death and bereavement in everyday conversation, has contributed to the spread of myths, assumptions and inaccuracies.

Grief counsellor and writer Dr Lois Tonkin refers to the 'new life' and subsequent adjustments after death, as growing your world *around* the deceased (Tonkin 2008). This is in opposition to the outdated notion that grief shrinks, diminishes or ends with time. Put simply: you do not 'get over it', you learn to live around it.

People who have not already experienced grief may expect a reduction in size and intensity over time. Imagine a bell jar with a large lump of coal in it. The perception is that over time the coal lump will reduce in size. In reality, the impact of grief and the attachment to the deceased remains, but the world around the loss expands in time. The bell jar will grow in dimension, whilst the large black lump (the grief) remains the same size (see Figure 1.1).

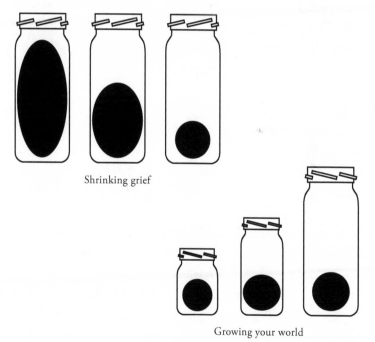

Shrinking grief

Growing your world

Figure 1.1: Growing your world around the grief

Ritualising continuing bonds can start as early as at the point of death, which is what the Victorians did by collecting hair samples of their loved ones to enclose into objects, particularly jewellery. Historically, memorialisation has waxed and waned depending on the cultural norm at the time. The last 20 years has seen a gradual increase in participation in memorialisation. Memorial benches, trees, flowers and rituals have become commonplace, but, in recent years, imaginative ways have been developed to memorialise ashes: pressing them into vinyl records, creating jewellery with ashes, adding them to ink prior to tattooing, adding them to paint before a portrait of the deceased has been created. There is even a company that will create fireworks with the ashes of loved ones. Together with alternative methods, the options related to whether to bury or cremate have also evolved significantly. This expansion of choice contributes to continuing bonds, either explicitly or implicitly.

Another model, developed in the 1990s, that fits perfectly with the continuing bonds view of grief is the Dual Process Model (Stroebe and Schut 1999). This model represents the moving back and forth between 'loss-orientation' and 'restoration-orientation'.

Loss-orientation entails focusing on the grief and the losses resulting from the death, and all the difficult elements within that process. Restoration-orientation is dealing with the changes that ensue and all the new things that should be broached. Put simply, it is the adjustment between looking backwards at the past, at life with the deceased, and accepting the loss, interspersed with looking forward to the future life without the loved one, and adjusting to life without them. It involves confronting the pain and loss, whilst also putting it to one side for periods of time.

Figure 1.2 demonstrates simply how this process occurs. The see-saw may be more heavily weighted in loss-orientation following the death, but with the processing of grief, eventually the griever's see-saw should tip more to restoration-orientation.

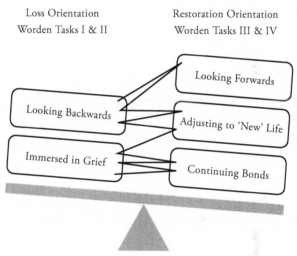

Figure 1.2: Visual demonstration of the Dual Process Model Figure (Stroebe and Schut 1999)

In the initial days after the death, grievers may sit in loss-orientation more than restoration-orientation, and as time progresses that balance may shift to the other direction. Death affects our identity, so, for example, if a husband dies after 50 years of marriage and he was cared for by his wife, she may struggle with the change in her identity from wife and carer to widow. Without the caring aspect of her life, how she spends her time will also be significantly impacted. The loss/restoration is clear to see in this example: as time goes on, other people and activities may fill in the time gaps, and her identity will reform, but no one will ever be able to replace her husband. That's why continuing bonds are important. They help us to maintain the relationship, but in another form, while we cope with the changes and the pain of the loved one's absence. This is another illustration of Tonkin's model of growing the world around the bereavement.

The Dual Process Model can also be aligned with Worden's tasks of mourning: with loss-orientation framed as accepting the reality of the loss and processing the pain of grief; and restoration-orientation framed as adjusting to a world without the deceased and finding an enduring connection.

Robert Neimeyer is another grief expert, who developed the concept of 'meaning making' as an important aspect of grief (Neimeyer and Sands 2011). He explains that to understand the unique experience of an individual's grief, it is useful to frame this within the context of the relationship's story.

For example, how does the death of a person's mother affect their life story? Prior to the death, the individual was moving in companionship, in one direction, with expectations of a future with the loved one. 'Meaning making' considers how the griever makes sense of their new, different future without that companionship and relationship. Neimeyer refers to the story of a person's life as a book. After a bereavement, the chapters yet to be written are ripped out of the book, and he likens this to the significance of the loss, with the physical presence of the loved one now gone. The aim of those supporting the bereaved is to allow the griever to build new meanings into life after death: 'a new narrative' (Neimeyer 2000). The construction of a new identity without this person can be a significant task and depends on the nature of the lost relationship and depth of the attachment.

There can be a search for identity meaning and who the griever is post-loss. This search for meaning is multi-faceted: for example, there are queries around death such as 'why' questions. Faith assumptions can be challenged, particularly after a child's death or a preventable death; there may be future purpose questions. The Dual Process Model can be overlaid onto meaning making to produce a more comprehensive picture of making sense of the past (loss-orientation), combined with meaning making for the future (restoration-orientation). The combination of the two models can represent how complicated grief can be and provide a clearer picture of the variables involved. For example, in the case of the death of an only child, parents can struggle with whether they are still labelled as 'mother' or 'father'. In this example, the meaning making will incorporate identity reconstruction in restoration-orientation.

Societies vary in cultural differences and the failure to recognise the loss of a significant attachment can lead to disenfranchised grief (Doka and Martin 2010). For example, in environments that do not recognise same-sex relationships, the death of a partner and the failure to recognise the significance of this by family and friends or society at large can have devastating effects on the bereaved. Grief that is unacknowledged, neglected, not expressed or avoided by others is all disenfranchised.

It could be argued that having a 'get over it' environment and expecting the bereaved to return to 'normal' life very quickly after a death can also lead to disenfranchisement. For example, it can be very difficult for a bereaved parent to return to work within days or even a few weeks after the death and be expected to carry on 'as normal'. Similarly, individuals who are left to live alone with little or no support could feel disenfranchised, so signposting to support organisations or support groups can be a lifeline to the facilitation of normal grieving patterns.

We can summarise that current grief models recognise:

- There are different types of losses suffered after the death of a significant attachment.

- The bereaved need to 'make sense' of the death of their loved one.

- The bereaved need to adjust to a life without the deceased.

- Continuous bonds are important.

- There is no right or wrong way to grieve.

- Grief is a unique and personal experience.

- Commonalities have been identified but don't apply to every person or every experience.

The physical and mental effects of grief

Whilst there is plenty of information on the emotional effects of grieving, very little has been written about the physical toll. As a result, this can be a surprise to grievers. The death of a loved one can be overwhelming, which may affect physical and mental health. While crying is commonly associated with grief, not everyone is prepared for potential digestive problems, chest tightness or pain, fatigue, tiredness, aches, forgetfulness, sleep pattern changes, concentration problems, anxiety, stress or depression, which may occur. Grief can exacerbate existing conditions and lead to increased symptoms.

The emotional impact of grief is well documented and the question of whether it is possible to die from a 'broken' heart has scientific roots. Grief can trigger the release of stress hormones that can lead to heart problems such as cardiovascular disease and cancer (Gupta 2015; Shear 2015).

This was supported by an American Heart Research study conducted to ascertain whether there was an increase in heart problems following a bereavement (Mostofsky *et al.* 2012). In the study, 1985 patients who were hospitalised following a heart attack (myocardial infarction) were analysed, and the researchers found that there was a 21 per cent increased risk of a reoccurrence for survivors within 24 hours following a significant bereavement. The risk remained six times higher than normal during the following week. These results confirm that grief following the death of a significant attachment contributes to an increased risk of heart problems immediately following the death. In other words: dying from a broken heart.

Further specific research was undertaken with partner bereavements for another study in 2014, which suggest that there was an increased risk of heart problems in the weeks following the death of a partner (Carey *et al.* 2014).

Other health problems have also been identified: a Swedish study found there was a correlation between Body Mass Index (BMI) and bereavement. BMI is the measure of body fat as a percentage of weight and height, and the higher the measure, the unhealthier this is deemed to be.

The results of the study showed an increase in BMI after the death of a parent (Oliveira *et al.* 2014). The report also includes the following statement:

> Losing a family member is one of life's most difficult experiences. Several studies have suggested that the death of a family member has an adverse effect on physical and mental health. It has also been revealed that bereavement has implications for mortality. For instance, Rostila et al. used a longitudinal design based on the total Swedish population register showed that the death of a child was associated with overall increased mortality in parents. They also found that the death of a parent was associated with children's mortality risk. Major explanations for the implications of bereavement for health involve increased chronic and acute stress and poor mental well-being.

Additionally, mental attitude to physical health can also be affected by bereavement. When someone's world has been shattered by grief, what could have been a normal ailment can sometimes be perceived as a serious life-threatening condition. The rationale of the conscious mind is that 'if it could happen to them, it could happen to me'; people can become much more aware of their own mortality after a bereavement.

In conclusion, the effects of grief are varied and there have been more developments in bereavement theory than tend to be commonly recognised.

Question: What is the worst kind of bereavement? Is it the death of a parent, a child, a friend, a colleague or a pet?

Answer: The death of a significant attachment.

Celebrant X was consulted to conduct a funeral ceremony for a deceased parent, who was universally disliked by the immediate family. This celebrant was quite shocked at the nature of the negative emotions towards the deceased, and was not sure how to proceed with the service.

Example of practical help: Celebrant X could spend time with the bereaved family members individually, and collectively, to ascertain what their needs are with regard to the funeral. It is ideal to understand the nature of each individual attachment, and the nature of the family dynamics, to provide a relevant and inclusive service. Recognising that the deceased person was not popular, it is still possible to conduct a service that is respectful of the position the deceased person held within the family (i.e. as the father/husband/grandfather).

Chapter 2

WHAT DO YOU SAY TO THE BEREAVED?

There are numerous platitudes and myths surrounding grief, some of which can be sensitive and respectful, others which can range from unhelpful to hurtful. Some people reply to the news of a bereavement with a platitude, in an attempt to reframe the grief, and make it appear manageable. Most people mean well, and are trying to be supportive and positive, but platitudes can be insensitive and cause emotional upset.

Language is a powerful tool and, used without consideration, can cause emotional and biological damage. Neuroscientists have determined that human brains tend to dwell on negativity (it's a survival mechanism), and any stressful event will exacerbate these thought processes. The more emotional a bereaved person is, the more tangible the imaginary becomes. Supporting with positive words and expressions can calm these thoughts and emotions for the griever, so they can feel more confident in their ability to cope (Newberg and Waldman 2013).

What not to say

The following are examples of the major variations of negative communication, platitudes, and unhelpful comments, followed by suggestions for more supportive reframing:

Variation No. 1 – Getting over it

'You will get over it'/'Are you over it yet?'/'You should be over it by now'

These are all inappropriate because they are either prescriptive or assumptive. We know from Chapter 1 that the myth that you 'get over it' stems from Freud during the war era. We now know from research that the bereaved learn to expand their world around the loss as time progresses, but the significance of the death, and subsequent losses, may not change regardless of time.

An alternative could be saying:

'Take your time'/'I am here for you whenever you need me'/'How are you today?'

Grief has no timeline. It has no prescribed limit, and some deaths are so significant they can affect the bereaved their entire lives. Every anniversary, every birthday of the deceased can be a painful reminder of the losses experienced. Unless there is an untreated incident of complicated grief (see Chapter 4), the acute grief will subside and become more manageable with time, but there is no proven timeline for this.

Variation No. 2 – Controlling grief

'What stage are you in?'/'You are in the X stage of grief'

These are both inappropriate, because as we have demonstrated in Chapter 1, grief does not follow a linear path through a set of prescribed stages. It is tempting to overlay grief with a sense of control, or try to 'benchmark' the process, but human reactions are more complex and unpredictable.

An alternative could be saying:

'I am here for you if you want to talk'/'Is there anything I can do for you?'/'Take your time'

It is enough to be supportive of the griever, whilst they fluctuate between loss-orientation and restoration-orientation, instead of trying to impose some order or expectation on them.

Variation No. 3 – Sympathy

'I know how you feel'/'You haven't grieved properly'/'My mother died too so I get it'

Everyone is an individual, with their own background, cultural norms, life stage, relationship, personalities, etc., and these variables integrate with another person's variables to create a unique relationship. The loss of that relationship, and the nature of the death, is unique and no one but that person knows how they feel. Even if you have had a similar bereavement, you will never know how that person feels, because you are not them. The bereaved may feel 'hijacked' if someone imposes their perception or personal experiences on them.

Sympathy is different from empathy, so well-wishers may be saying, 'I know how you feel', with the intention of offering support and understanding, without realising they are ambushing the bereaved person's story. Empathy is trying to understand what the other person is feeling whilst relating it to how you may have felt in a similar or imagined situation.

An alternative could be saying:

> 'I don't know how you feel but I am here for you'/'I don't know what your loss is like for you, but if you'd like to talk'/'Would you like to talk?'

The bereaved generally require recognition, and emotional and/or practical support. They want reassurance that you understand the impact of their losses. Empathy is important because the more you listen, the more you will hear, and the better you will be able to support that person.

Don't be afraid to ask the griever about the loved one, it will not 'upset' them, they are already 'upset'. Most grievers welcome the opportunity to share their memories.

Variation No. 4 – Judgement

> 'Don't cry'/'You shouldn't feel angry'/'S/he wouldn't want you to say/do that'

Grief is a natural and normal event, and part of that process can involve feelings of guilt or anger, or both. All feelings are normal for that person, and should be supported without judgement.

An alternative could be saying:

> 'How are you feeling today?'

Crying is a normal physical reaction to grief and should not be discouraged. Telling someone not to cry, or that their deceased loved one wouldn't want them to cry, undermines their feelings and their natural response. Do not be afraid of silence if the griever is crying. There can be a temptation to fill the silence with words but there is no need, the bereaved need space to process their emotions and thoughts, and silence allows that.

Variation No. 5 – Comparison

'My grief is worse than yours because...'

There is an innate 'hierarchy' of grief that involves comparing relationships. Chapter 1 highlighted that the depth of the relationship, and the significance of the loss, are what matters most, not simply the 'label' of the relationship. For example, a bereaved widow who was married for 30 years might feel her grief is 'deeper' than that of someone who has been married two years, but that view would be based on many assumptions that may be groundless.

An alternative could be saying:

'I was so sad to hear about X'/'You are in my thoughts'

No one knows how someone else is feeling. What may be an insignificant loss to one person, could be a devastating loss to someone else, and this should be respected, regardless of how the relationship might be labelled: mother, friend, sister, brother, child, etc. The 'label' still denotes hierarchy and attitudes within society in general. For example, it is assumed that every child has a strong attachment and close relationship with their mother, but this is not always the case. In the event of someone's mother dying, there is usually a lot of empathy and support for the bereaved person, but they might not have had a close relationship. In some cases, the children might not have had any contact with their mother at all. These children may have a deep love for their stepmother, in the absence of a relationship with their mother. In this case, their loss will be significant when the stepmother dies, but may not be as significant when the mother dies. It is important not to assume an understanding of the relationship just from the label, in this case 'mother' vs. 'stepmother'.

Hierarchies also exist due to a need for grief to be recognised. Where once Victorians denoted their mourning status outwardly, through their clothing and adornments, social media and online platforms are now allowing free expressions of grief again. Within this public environment, jostling for positions of grieving 'importance' are evident. For example, a grieving widow may resent friends setting up a memorial site for her husband, feeling that she should be the one to do so.

Variation No. 6 – Clichés

'They are in a better place now'/'They aren't suffering any more'

Everyone has their own personal beliefs on what happens after death, but the griever may want more than anything to have that person back. These platitudes may be interpreted to mean that the deceased is better off out of the griever's life.

An alternative could be saying:

> 'I was so sad to hear of the death of X, is there anything I can do?'/'How are you feeling today?'

Both platitudes only highlight the losses that have occurred, it is better to acknowledge the death and express empathy to support the griever.

Variation No. 7 – Sorry

> 'I'm sorry for your loss'

This has become a standard statement that most people use; for most it is a comfort, but for some it is an irritant. This carries a warning because not everyone wants to hear that you are 'sorry' or have the impact of the death reduced to the word 'loss'. Whilst it is true that there are losses when someone dies, *the person is not physically 'lost'; they will not be found.*

This has become a culturally normal expression of sympathy, and is mostly received with acceptance, but some people welcome more direct or creative sentiments.

An alternative could be saying:

> 'I'm sorry for the rubbish time you're having right now'/'My sincere condolences to you'

As a friend, family member or professional supporting the bereaved, our expressions need be appropriate for the circumstances and the nature of the relationship we have with them. If the normal relationship language involves a more direct approach, or a more formal tone, there really is no need to deviate.

Variation No. 8 – Every cloud has a silver lining

'You can always have more children'

This is arguably the worst thing you can possibly say to a bereaved parent, whether due to miscarriage or stillbirth or through to the death of a baby or older child. There are several reasons why this is inappropriate, including the fact that they may not be able to have more children. Additionally, this comment could be interpreted in a manner that suggests that the embryo/baby/child that has died can be replaced.

An alternative could be saying:

'I'm thinking of you'/'What can I do?'

Nobody can predict the future.

Variation No. 9 – Life carries on

'Now that the funeral is over, you can get back to your normal life'

Life after a death becomes split into two parts: before they died and after they died. Life does not ever 'go back to the way it was'. Additionally, what is not always appreciated is that there are often secondary losses after a death. These vary considerably and can include practical elements such as the loss of income and resulting financial losses. There can also be social losses such as the loss of social life, loss of identity and loss of support. There can be cognitive losses, such as the loss of confidence, goals and aspirations. There can also be a shattering of the assumptive world, which can also lead to a loss of faith. For example, in the case of a child's death, every parent assumes they will outlive their child, so there can be a rejection of a 'God' or higher being for 'doing this to me'. The future as it was imagined is now the past. Secondary losses are inexhaustible, and can be significant in their impact on the life of the bereaved when they are already in an emotionally vulnerable state.

An alternative could be to say:

'What can I do to help you?'/'What do you need?'/'Can I do anything?'/'I will be in touch to see how you are'

Whilst most people do resume regular activities, some time after the funeral, this will not be a return to 'normal life' for them. The bereaved will often have lessening support as time goes by, and this is when a follow-up phone call, a note or a meeting will have most impact. For professionals interacting with the griever around the time of bereavement, it would be useful to help them identify where their sources of support are likely to be. The newly bereaved liken grief to being in a 'fog', so even the simplest of thought processes or decisions may be difficult for them. A Further Resources directory is included at the end of this book.

Variation No. 10 – At least...

'At least they died doing something they loved'

The words 'at least' should never precede a comment to a bereaved person. It undermines everything they are feeling and experiencing. Language is such a contentious issue because grievers can be sensitive and emotional, particularly immediately after the death.

An alternative could be to say:

'I know how much they loved to…'

Acknowledging the cause of death is not insensitive if it is recognising something they were passionate about, and done in an empathic, supportive way.

Giving the right support

People can be unsure about what to say, and platitudes are usually well intentioned. Observations anecdotally, and on social media, demonstrate a consensus that it is better to say something than to say nothing at all. The bereaved may feel aggrieved if their status as a mourner is ignored. In some cases, this can lead to disenfranchised grief, which is where grief is not perceived to be acknowledged by society.

Grievers don't always know what they need, or want, or how to articulate this, which can make it even more difficult for others to interpret. In addition, some people who are interacting with them such as family, friends and co-workers don't necessarily know what to say or do. When you put these two dynamics together, it is inevitable that misunderstandings arise and platitudes are used.

Consideration should be given to people who are grieving collectively, such as families who have experienced the death of a family member. Each of them had their own relationship with the deceased, have their own personality and life experiences, and their own 'role' within the family.

The term 'holding space' is particularly relevant with the bereaved; offering non-judgemental support in an empathic way, allowing silence, allowing emotions, listening attentively and being genuinely present with them.

Another myth is that everyone requires counselling after a bereavement. Research rejects the need for counselling for normal grief because, by definition, it is a *normal* event with *normal* responses. Schut *et al.* (2001) found that professional intervention may be harmful for those who are normally bereaved. Bereavement support groups or counselling can be beneficial for some because counsellors are specially trained to listen and empathise, but they are not *necessary* for everyone.

Resilience determines how individuals react to adverse events psychologically, so is an important aspect of grief. Whilst many people struggle with adverse life events and need support following a death, some people appear to cope better. George Bonanno, an academic at Columbia University, USA, has researched loss and trauma extensively over the past 20 years and states:

> …large numbers of people manage to endure the temporary upheaval of loss or potentially traumatic events remarkably well, with no apparent disruption in their ability to function at work or in close relationships, and seem to move on to new challenges with apparent ease. (Bonanno 2004, p.20)

Language is an emotive issue and what comforts one person may be perceived as a platitude to another. But the overarching message should be this: it is better to say something than to say nothing at all. Being supportive, and providing an environment where the griever can utilise their resilience, provides a much-needed safety net.

Consider why the following are different:

1. The death of a child.

2. Death within the family structure.

3. Death by suicide.

4. The death of a partner/spouse.

5. The death of a parent.

6. Death by road accident.

7. How death impacts on older people.

By considering the examples above, you can explore the nuances that bereaved people may experience. Here are some examples:

1. The death of a child is unique, because it is the death of the dreams the parent had, and the future that they imagined. It is also unique because it is the only relationship between two people where one person created the other. All other relationships are formed externally. The death of a child is also an out of order death: parents are expected to die before their children, whether they are still in gestation or adult children.

2. Family structures are complicated, and even more so in extended families. There are assumptions of roles and expectations that may or may not be met after a bereavement. Each family member will react to the death and grieve in their own way. The attachment to the deceased will vary with each person, despite being within the same family. Conflict can arise if family members think they are 'more' bereaved than others.

There may also be expectations of the role the family members will take with regard to the funeral and who will be making the decisions. Resentment and blaming can occur if the family are not communicating effectively, and this will have a residual effect on any children or young people. Every effort should be made to ensure families communicate with each other and include children (in an age-appropriate way).

3. Suicide presents challenges because the overriding question is always 'Why?', whether there is a note left by the bereaved or not. Guilt is a common emotion experienced by the survivors, due to the 'what if' scenarios. Social stigma remains in some environments, and the griever may therefore feel isolated or unsupported. When interacting with someone affected by suicide, it is important to remember that they are still bereaved primarily, the nature of the death should not be the focus.

4. The death of a partner/spouse can be overwhelming, not only because of the emotional loss, but also because it leads to secondary losses. These can be financial if the deceased was the sole earner, or if the bereaved is unable to work following the death. These can be practical losses: if the deceased was the carer, driver, etc. There can be a loss of identity: for example, the status change from 'married' to 'widowed'. There can also be other losses such as loss of faith or support. There is also the loss of the future – many couples plan for holidays or retirement together, for example. The death may also lead to the loss of security or confidence. There can also be social and/or friendship losses. There may

be loneliness, and living within the home full of memories may be difficult.

5. The death of a parent, step-parent or carer can be a considerable loss, particularly when that person has been there from birth or infanthood. As they may have provided the role of unconditional love, support and stability, losing that can lead to complicated feelings. There can be a feeling of abandonment, and it can also make people aware of their own mortality when they become the eldest generation. There may also be a shift in family dynamics, particularly when the last surviving parent dies. There may also be a provocation of sibling rivalry and tensions between family members.

6. Road deaths are premature, sudden and traumatic. They are widely reported in the press, which can also impact on the bereaved. They are the result of someone else's action or inaction so there is a causation factor that can give rise to blame and anger. Road deaths involve police investigations and legal processes. These processes and complications can be stressful for the family and can be confusing and overwhelming to manage.

7. Some older people become unable to cope with the impact of death, particularly when it is a lifelong spouse or one of their children, for example. Many elderly people are dependent on others for tasks, and for the quality of their life and when that person dies it has a significant impact. They may be living alone for the first time in their adult life and this may leave them feeling lonely and isolated. They may have lost the person who shares the most memories with them, and this

can affect their sense of identity. Some older people may feel that they have lost everything from their past, with a bleak future ahead. Death for older people can also signal a sense of their own mortality, particularly following multiple bereavements.

Chapter 3

AN INTRODUCTION TO GRIEVING STYLES

The uniqueness of human beings

Everyone is a unique individual who reacts and responds to life events in different ways. As this applies to everything that happens during our lifetime, bereavement is no exception. In 2016 there were a lot of high-profile and surprising celebrity deaths and bereavements. As a result, there has been an increase in articles published on bereavement, and an increase in books available, either with collective bereavement stories or one person's story. Whilst this information is interesting and can be insightful, it can also be detrimental to read another person's story and 'benchmark' against it. Comparison is inevitable, and whilst there can be common themes, every person and every experience is different.

Individuals rarely live in isolation; they are part of a network of friends and family that interacts with each layer of society. These may include national bereavement-related laws, organisational bereavement policies, support from local organisations, through to the interaction with family and friends. This is a far-reaching web of variables ranging from the global level encompassing the internet, through to the individual level of personal relationships. These various levels of interaction provide potential complications that may affect the griever.

Family dynamics are also particularly relevant to the bereaved following a death as they usually influence funeral wishes and memorialisation. It can be a surprise to other family members to find out that the legal executor and next of kin are able to make all decisions.

Introvert and extrovert personality types

For simplicity, other variations of personality types are excluded, and this chapter will concentrate on assuming that everyone is generally introverted or extroverted.

Introverts are individuals who generally tap into their inward resources for strength and grounding. Extroverts, conversely, tend to generate energy from interacting with others. This does not necessarily mean introverts are shy or non-social, or that extroverts don't enjoy time alone.

The bereaved will generally grieve within the same pattern of behaviour that they exhibit prior to the death. For example, when an introverted person who prefers to spend a lot of time at home is bereaved, it would be expected that they would grieve at home. Complications arise when others expect this person to grieve socially, for example, expecting that they should join a support group. The key word here is 'expect'.

Conversely, an extroverted person who spends a lot of time socialising may seek support from the friends that they are socialising with, within the same environment.

By doing so they are not 'avoiding' grief, but exhibiting their natural behaviour and grieving in their own way.

Intuitive and instrumental grieving types

Another useful approach to consider is whether someone is an intuitive or an instrumental griever (Doka and Martin 2010). Intuitive grievers share their emotions either physically or verbally, through crying or talking about how they are feeling. Intuitive grievers experience grief in an acute way, and are frequently represented in the arts as anguished and crying. This can cause non-intuitive grievers to question if they are 'doing it right' because they grieve differently.

The bloggers pouring their hearts out on the internet, the bereaved writing about their anguish in newspapers, autobiographical books and magazines, are all intuitive grievers who gain strength and support from openly expressing their emotions. Not all intuitive grievers express themselves publicly, some express themselves privately, but all of them need to express their emotions to validate and 'work through' their grief. 'This retelling the story and re-enacting the pain is a necessary part of grieving and an integral part of the intuitive pattern of grieving' (Doka and Martin 2010, p.38). They may experience more physical symptoms, such as exhaustion or confusion, because all their energy is directed at grieving.

Instrumental grievers deal with bereavement through trying to make sense of what has happened; events determine their thoughts and actions. The focus for instrumental grievers is on problem-solving, and on the desire to contain their feelings. These are intellectual processes, utilising thoughts to channel their grief, rather than the emotional displays of an intuitive griever. It can be a misconception that their lack of expression of emotions represents a lack of grieving. They simply grieve in a different way. Instrumental grievers share common feelings experienced by intuitive grievers, such as sadness, anxiety, loneliness and yearning (see Worden 2010). What is different is the strength of these feelings. For the intuitive griever, feelings are intense, whereas for the instrumental griever, they are not as overwhelming.

Doka and Martin's research, which I have drawn on in this section, was an exploration of the differences between male and female grieving patterns, and found more women tended to be intuitive and more men tended to be instrumental. However, not all men are instrumental and not all women are intuitive. Over time, with successive generations, the socialisation of girls and boys has been converging, as shown in Figure 3.1. Whilst gender differences remain within society, many people now hold non-stereotypical gender roles. Women are now largely active in the workplace, in occupations historically undertaken by men, and many men are now primary caregivers. These changes blur the lines of sex expectations, and in turn allow individuals to express themselves in a more authentic way, rather than sometimes dictated by society. However, this is still a slow evolution.

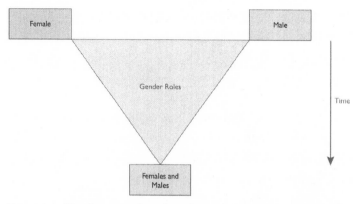

Figure 3.1: The changing of gender roles within society over time

Differences between instrumental and intuitive grievers can give rise to misunderstandings, with either believing the other may not be grieving 'properly' because they do not exhibit the same grieving style. The same can be said of introverts and extroverts, who may believe that the other 'should' be doing what they are doing, to grieve 'properly'.

Grievers can be anywhere on the spectrum between introverts and extroverts, and can also be anywhere on the spectrum of intuitive or instrumental grieving styles. It is also possible to move between the two. The variables are not mutually exclusive, and blending is common. The combination of these basic four categories provides the following framework:

- *Extrovert/intuitive*: Feelings are felt intensely and expressed publicly.

- *Introvert/intuitive*: Feelings are felt intensely and expressed privately.

- *Extrovert/instrumental*: Thinking is expressed physically and publicly.

- *Introvert/instrumental*: Thinking is expressed physically and privately.

In each of these categories there is a sliding scale, the middle range of which is called *ambivert*. From this framework alone, there are many variables that determine a unique grieving style for each person. Note that these categories are simply indicators of what someone *could* be experiencing, and are intended to describe the differences. They are not intended to be prescriptive.

Generally, people grieve in the way they expressed themselves prior to the death, but grief can also change people, and this should not be underestimated. For example, an active, extroverted young mother may become more introverted after the death of her child. Grievers can move back and forth along the scales, and can also change style with different bereavements. For example, someone may grieve in an intuitive way with a particular death. For example, someone may grieve in an instrumental way for their parents, but grieve in an intuitive way after the death of their child. Over a lifetime, people can also change and move up and down the scale depending on circumstances, and their lives can completely change after a significant attachment loss. For example, a widower who was previously introverted, preferring to spend most of his time at home with his wife, may spend more time outside the home, with other people, after her death.

Social aspects of grieving

Whilst it is helpful to look at the individual griever, wider aspects of society also influence and shape experiences. Urie Bronfenbrenner, a psychologist, developed a model demonstrating the ecological systems surrounding individuals (Bronfenbrenner and Morris 2007). These include:

- *The Microsystem*: This is the system closest to the individual, and includes family and friends.

- *The Mesosystem*: This is slightly removed, and includes neighbours and work colleagues.

- *The Exosystem*: This is the next level, and includes the mass media and local politics.

- *The Macrosystem*: This is the cultural environment that the individual and their systems exist within, for example global politics, history and the internet.

Figure 3.2 is a simplified depiction of the griever immersed in the global world, whilst surrounded by family and friends. The interactions of different ecosystems can be simple or complex: they can involve employers, benefit agencies, schools, support systems, charities, funeral directors, celebrants, churches, etc. Some grievers utilise their support system as an emotional or physical 'fortress' to buffer them whilst they are grieving, whereas others grieve independently and interact with other ecological systems alone.

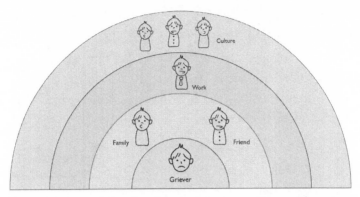

Figure 3.2: Some of the griever's ecological systems (Rustam Eltman)

Within the various ecological systems, society has expectations of the bereaved, and perceptions of behaviour. In every support group I have facilitated, I have observed what I call a 'hierarchy' of grief, where a form of benchmarking occurs between participants. Premature deaths and the death of a child seem to 'rank' higher than deaths of older people from natural causes. Suicide sits awkwardly within the ranking, due to the nature of the death and because of the perceived 'preventability' factor. *All deaths are not considered equal.*

Attachment theory

As mentioned in Chapter 1, another variable that affects grief is the person's attachment style. Attachment theory, first proposed by John Bowlby, can influence the impact of the death on the bereaved person.

An American-Canadian developmental psychologist, Mary Ainsworth (1973), progressed Bowlby's identification of the emotional attachment we have with others, through observing the behaviour of young children. She identified three types of attachment, and these relate to differing responses to grief:

- *Secure*: This is where children are emotionally balanced and have parents who are responsive to their needs. Grievers with secure attachments will adjust normally to grief. They should either have a network of support to access, or the ability to find relevant support and resources.

- *Avoidant*: This is where children who have parents that are neglectful of their needs so they are forced to become independent. These grievers may not demonstrate their needs and may appear to be coping without any outside support.

- *Anxious-ambivalent*: This is where children have parents who are unreliable in responding to their needs so they become 'needy'. These grievers may be overly dependent on their friends, family or external sources to carry them through their grief process. They may demonstrate their emotions more overtly and may feel that the depth of their emotions may not be recognised.

This research on attachment styles allows us to understand the type of emotional connection someone has in relationships, because of what has been demonstrated to them. Children will learn from behaviours and relationship patterns that their parents show, and their expectations of what behaviours and relationships 'should' be like are heavily influenced by these. Further research suggests that attachment styles continue throughout the lifespan, for example in romantic relationships (Hazan and Shaver 1987).

The combination of the introvert/extrovert, intuitive/ instrumental, attachment style and ecological systems demonstrate the different personality types, grieving types and social typology that an individual will be affected by after a death. These are all useful indicators of what someone may be experiencing, but are by no means exhaustive. When the relationship with the deceased, the interaction of the two personalities and the social and cultural background, are also considered, it is clear to see why each bereavement is unique. Even *normal* grief can be complex.

Take a moment to think about whether you are an introvert, extrovert or ambivert. Next think about whether you are an instrumental or intuitive griever. Now take a moment to think about all the bereavements that you have experienced and how you and others interacted following them.

When supporting a bereaved person, it may be helpful to ascertain their personality type, and grieving type, to enable a more suitable approach to support. The following is just a guideline but may be helpful:

- *Introvert/instrumental*: May find it difficult to explain how they are feeling, and may be more comfortable expressing in practical ways. They may find organising the funeral from the safety of their home, and undertaking paperwork online, are effective for their grieving style. As they may prefer to be alone, it might be best to offer support, and send useful links to websites, or offer to visit them when it is convenient for them.

- *Introvert/intuitive*: May find it difficult to deal with the practical arrangements, and interact with external organisations because they express emotionally. They may find themselves crying, or attempting to prevent becoming emotional whilst on phone calls and in similar situations. The best way to support this person might be to offer practical support: walk the dog, babysit, drive them somewhere, be with them when they must interact in public. As above, they recharge alone, so offer to help, but allow them to accept it in their own time, on their own terms.

- *Extrovert/instrumental*: May prefer support outside of the home, with other people. They may be found joining organisations or support groups. The best way to support them might be to arrange to meet them publicly or attend activities with them.

- *Extrovert/intuitive*: May recharge outside of the home, but rather than as 'doers', they may want to engage in activities that involve talking and expressing their feelings. They may benefit from bereavement support groups or other social gatherings where they are able to express their emotions. They may blog or publicly express their emotions via social media, in newspaper articles or write a book. The best way to support them might be to listen to their stories.

Digital grieving

An added complication of modern life is the rapid evolution of the internet. This medium can blur the boundaries for extroverts and introverts. Introverts can post online from the safety of their home, and extroverts have a much wider audience. Whereas behaviour offline can be relatively predictable, social media and blogging have exposed introverts to external communication methods, and extroverts have access to new audiences.

When considering all the variables; whether introvert, extrovert, intuitive or instrumental, and the blended combinations, there is a forum online that caters for everyone. There are a multitude of blogs written by intuitive grievers, whether extrovert or introvert, as they can write from a personal space (e.g. at home) or a public space (e.g. in a café). Self-published books by grievers, counselling books, magazines and newspapers are full of stories of intuitive personalities expressing their emotions. Instrumental grievers could typically be expected to set up memorial websites, or conduct research.

While more obvious in physical situations, the 'hierarchy' of grief may not be as evident on social media. The family – the 'chief' – mourners may feel they should have complete control over the messaging online. However, others may post without understanding that this dynamic exists. Social cues are evident when we are interacting at funerals: immediate family sit at the front and those with the 'lesser' relationships sit or stand at the back. Within the online world, these cues are not obvious or stated.

Digital legacies

Social media and the internet have changed society completely. The bereavement experience and grief have therefore been significantly affected too. These add another layer of complications, not only in ascertaining the extent of the digital legacy and deciding what can be done with each strand, but they also increase the emotional toll. For example, gaining access to bank accounts, deleting online accounts and managing or deleting social media accounts can all be time-consuming and overwhelming emotionally.

The digital world is such a new and rapidly expanding area, that it can be confusing and legally challenging. Each organisation has their own rules, and countries vary on their treatment of online content after death. A further complication is the fear of losing data (e.g. emails, text messages or digital photographs). Online backups and storage solutions are available, and should be signposted to the bereaved, to preserve any precious digital inheritance. Digital legacies are theoretically no different to inheriting a filing cupboard full of overflowing files, except the deceased might not have had legal ownership of some of them. To appreciate the scope of increasing platforms, these can include: social media sites, online creative sites for music, online banking, email accounts, smartphones, online shopping accounts, to name a few. The list is growing rapidly as we become more digitalised. Some of the content may be copyright protected and remain the property of the deceased, but that does not automatically ensure there are inheritance rights. Some of the content is owned by the online service provider, and will not pass to the next of kin.

Online memorials

Prior to the internet, memorials were restricted to physical objects, such as headstones and notices in newspapers. Memorialisation can now include online memorial sites and social media pages. Families may have differing opinions on what is appropriate online memorialisation, what is not, and how to deal with the inherited legacy. Another complication is that anyone can theoretically post anything publicly online, without consultation or consent. This can be particularly problematic with social media sites, and stories of parents learning about the death of their child through a post have been reported.

This is a complex area that is still developing and evolving legally, which may cause confusion and added stress for the bereaved. Acceptable practice, and laws, will normalise and stabilise over time, but in the meantime the complications should be acknowledged.

Grief and the internet

The internet permeates every aspect of modern lives, and technology has transformed our engagement with death, dying and bereavement.

Figure 3.3: The global impact of the internet

We have already looked at the three main areas of the internet that affect the bereaved: digital legacies, online mourning and memorialisation, but because of the widespread use of online resources, and the pace of the increase in technology, there are various areas that also demand careful consideration whilst supporting grievers:

- *Digital legacy*: One area that the law has been slow to respond to concerns the digital legacy someone left behind. This can include social media sites, online accounts such as bank accounts, content stored online such as music and photographs, blogs, registered domains, online selling or buying accounts such as Amazon or eBay, email accounts, loyalty cards, the list can be endless. The bereaved may not have access to these accounts, or know they exist, which can lead to further complications, particularly if they are not digitally literate. Some online content may not be owned by the deceased, for example they may have a licence from the host company. What happens to the information, or content, after death will depend on the administering organisation. Some organisations will require the next of kin to provide information, and a copy of the death certificate, before they will engage in correspondence over inherited online content.

- *Online support*: An internet search will reveal many individuals worldwide who write about their own, or other people's individual grief experiences. Some of these may be helpful, but caution should be exercised not to 'benchmark' or compare because every grief experience is unique. Many people give advice that may apply to them personally, or others they know, but the information may not be appropriate for someone else.

- *Digital immortality*: There are several companies that provide services which claim to provide an eternal avatar of a person. They claim the thoughts and stories of someone can be preserved and perpetuated for eternity. Technology is changing at a rapid pace, so the preservation of all digital content may not be possible in the future. Whether these services support the bereaved, or prolong grief (in the case of the creation of an avatar of the deceased) will depend on individual perspective. Death is final, grief is normal, and continuing bonds are important, so the introduction of technology in this area should be ethical and considered.

- *Online bereavement etiquette*: Social media is a powerful medium for spreading messages and demonstrating public displays of emotion. The hierarchy of grief has no better platform than this: the immediate family are easily offended by posts that they have not sanctioned and, worse, finding out a loved one has died via a social media post can be devastating. In the absence of a specific memorial website, private messaging may be more appropriate for grief expressions, until a precedent has been set by the digital inheritor. Tagging the deceased person in posts may appear on the family's and friends' feeds, which could cause distress. The younger generation may not be as aware of these issues as the pre-internet generation, because they have grown up within a publicly expressive world.

- *Online memorialisation*: There are many sites worldwide that are set up to enable the bereaved to create a memorial to their loved one. These very often include photos and words that facilitate continuing bonds in a digital age. Social media can also be utilised in the same way, leading to the phenomenon of the *digital zombie* – the dead who remain 'alive' in a digital world (Bassett 2015). Social media allow the dead to remain in the present.

Digital legacy information (correct at time of going to press)
Facebook

Facebook offers the option of a legacy contact who can manage an account in the event of a bereavement, but this person must be selected prior to the death. The legacy contact will be able to respond to new friend requests, update profile and cover pictures, and write pinned posts. They will not be able to log in to the account, read messages, remove existing friends, or alter any past content posted on the page.

If no legacy contact was nominated prior to the death, Facebook has a FAQ section that provides information on the two options available: memorialising the account, or deleting the account. Memorialising the account means that the page will remain, and confirmed friends can leave comments. Facebook will not share the login information so the account is completely secured. Deleting the account means that all the content and information will be completely removed. If someone has tagged the deceased in a picture, that will remain but all pictures originating with the deceased will be deleted.

Twitter

Twitter does not operate legacy contact or memorialisation schemes; the only option available is to delete the account. This can only be undertaken by a verified family member of the deceased, or the executor of the estate. Once the request has been submitted, Twitter will request identity verification and a copy of the death certificate.

Instagram

Instagram allows the memorialisation or removal of an account. Despite being owned by Facebook, they do not allow the nomination of a legacy contact. Details of the login information will not be released, and the account is secured.

LinkedIn

LinkedIn requires a family member or executor to provide the member's name, URL for the profile, relationship to the deceased, the date of death and the company they most recently worked for. The profile will then be deleted; they do not memorialise accounts.

As technology evolves, the web of digitalisation will become more embedded within everyday life. This means the internet will become increasingly more important in legacy planning, dying, rituals, grieving, meaning making, and continuing bonds.

Chapter 4

IS GRIEF 'TRAUMATIC' OR A MENTAL HEALTH PROBLEM?

Previous chapters have referred to *normal* grief. This is the normal process of adjusting to the death, and any other related losses. There are other variations of grief, including anticipatory, complicated and traumatic, which are explored further in this chapter.

Due to the complexity of grief, and the complicated nature of individuals, it is difficult to determine finite definitions of *normal*. Every grief expression, and the understanding of it, is relative to individual experience and perspective. The guidance provided to professionals on deviations from normal grief, and the interpretation of this information, can be variable and controversial. In general, *complicated grief* is an umbrella term for pathological grief, or any deviation from 'normal'.

It should be noted that the definitions within this area are subject to continuous variations and changes. The guidelines for what constitutes 'normal' and 'complicated' stem from the American Psychiatric Association's *Diagnostic and Statistical Manual of Mental Disorders* (DSM-x).

Each version of the DSM has updated diagnostic criteria, and bereavement has had various evolutions. For example, in the DSM-IV, it was stated that grief was distinct and separate from a depression diagnosis. This was changed in the current DSM-5 so that depressive symptoms following a death can be diagnosed as depression.

Anticipatory grief is a type of normal, and is not pathological. It is the process of grieving before the person has died, experiencing sadness, loss and other feelings associated with grief prior to the death. Anticipatory grief is common when a loved one is living with a degenerative illness such as dementia, the griever witnesses the changes to, and disappearance of, the person as they knew them. It can also occur following the diagnosis of a terminal illness, as family and friends prepare for the death, and life without that person.

Unlike normal grief, and the gradual adjustment of rebuilding life around the losses, anticipatory grief lasts whilst the loved one is alive. Therefore, this can be a prolonged experience.

When death is sudden, there may be a traumatic response experienced by the bereaved. The effect of the traumatic element *may* lead to complicated grief. A sudden death such as suicide, murder or road death also has the added complication of involvement with the police, the coroner, the courts and the media. These additional factors, together with the traumatic element, add additional stressors that may lead to complicated grief. This does not mean that everyone bereaved with a sudden and/or traumatic element will experience complicated grief. Perception, resilience, circumstances, personality and support are all critical elements that contribute to bereavement outcomes. The trauma is just one variable of the many complexities involved.

Complicated grief

The adjustment period following a death can take varying lengths of time, and as we know from Lois Tonkin (2008; see Chapter 1), the loss does not diminish, the bereaved simply grow their world around it. Acute feelings of grief are common immediately following the death, but they lessen in their severity over time. Complicated grief is the umbrella term for when this does not happen.

We have already explored why grief may be ordinarily complicated, due to the variables involved; both individually and socially. Therefore the 'diagnosis' of 'complicated' grief is contentious. One perspective might argue that bereavement is fundamentally complex and believe that variations from normal grief are natural. When there is a failure to grow the world around the loss, adaptation is the problem, not the grief, and this is referred to as complicated grief.

'The Usher', Monoprint (2011) by Alysia Trackim:
'My work investigates complicated grief through
meaning-making, self-narrative, and absent-presence...'

Those who do not subscribe to 'complicated' grief as a separate entity to 'normal' grief, believe the lack of reorganisation is due to the bereaved feeling unsupported, and/or having little resilience, and/or lacking recognition of the grief, and that this can be rectified through support, building resilience and recognition.

Despite varying views from academics on whether grief can be pathological or not, Stroebe *et al.* (2017) state, 'Grief is not a disease but bereavement merits medical awareness.'

Complicated grief as an illness

For those that believe complicated grief is a separate entity to normal grief, it is estimated that approximately 10 per cent of bereaved people will develop it (Delaney 2016). There are various definitions of complicated grief, and the American Psychiatric Association's *Diagnostic and Statistical Manual of Mental Disorders* (DSM-5) states that it can be diagnosed as Persistent Complex Bereavement Disorder (PCBD), which Parkes (2014, p.287) defines as 'Adjustment Disorder following the death of a loved one when the intensity, quality, or persistence of grief reactions exceeds what normally might be expected, when cultural, religious, or age-appropriate norms are taken into account.' According to Parkes (2014), PCBD has commonalities that include:

- suicide risk

- deficits in work and social functioning

- harmful health behaviours

- marked increases in risk of serious medical conditions

- reduced quality of life.

Another characterisation of complex grief is Prolonged Grief Disorder (PGD), which was identified by Prigerson and colleagues (2009). PGD results from a sudden, premature, and traumatic death. This type of complicated grief was explained earlier in this chapter. Traumatic grief has similar indicators to post-traumatic stress disorder (PTSD), which can include:

- intrusive memories, flashbacks and/or nightmares

- intense physical, emotional and psychological reactions to reminders of the event

- sleep disorders and alcohol/substance abuse

- difficulty concentrating and irritability

- feeling detached, and/or having a complete lack of interest in activities

- re-experiencing the event (feeling like it was 'yesterday' despite the passage of time).

The traumatic element is different to grief. This is due to the brain being unable to process the event normally, which may lead the person to feel that they can't make sense of their emotions. Some people with PGD state that they feel one thing, but are thinking another. For example, they may *feel* that they could have done something to prevent a suicide, but their *thoughts* recognise there was nothing they could have done (it is acknowledged that CBT would argue that these are both thoughts, but that is outside of the scope of this book).

Despite the different definitions of PGD and PCBD, in 2016 Prigerson and colleagues published a research paper stating they believe the two have insignificant differences (Maciejewski *et al.* 2016). Critics argue that their inclusion in the *DSM* inappropriately medicalises grief.

The definitions of complicated grief can therefore be confusing with the variety of labels. PGD, PCBD, 'traumatic' grief, 'disenfranchised' grief and 'carried' grief are all examples of different variations. 'Complicated grief' is being used in this book as an umbrella term.

Despite disagreement over whether grief can in fact be considered a mental illness (Dreher 2013), it is generally accepted that complicated grief is intense and prolonged, with a debilitating effect that is chronic and does not diminish over time (Shear 2006; Worden 2010).

Research has concluded that complicated grief occurs more in women than men, and whilst symptoms may appear within a short time after the death, the full spectrum of symptoms may be delayed by years (Parkes 2014). Therefore, it is possible that following a subsequent bereavement, the griever may have complicated grief from a previous loss.

Complicated impact

The inability to grieve normally can be a response to many issues:, including a dysfunctional attachment style, absence of support, a conflicted or abusive relationship, a premature death, a sudden or traumatic death, personality type, lack of resilience, It can also be due to previous experiences. These variables will affect our grieving process. Just as normal grief varies from person to person, the same influences also compound complicated grief.

Here are three simplified examples of complicated grief variations:

- *Chronic/prolonged grief* arises where the initial chronic emotions, and reactions do not diminish over time. There is no gradual adjustment to life after the loss.

- *Delayed/carried grief* arises when the normal reactions to a death occur much later than is typical. These have been inhibited, so if grief does exhibit at a later stage, they may seem excessive or unrelated to the bereavement.

- *Disenfranchised grief* occurs when grief isn't or can't be socially recognised. Examples may include pet death (not considered 'significant' by some), grief from abortion or miscarriage, grief from the death of an ex-partner, or grief experienced by someone following the death of a married lover.

Normal grief can be intense and painful and may last much longer than Western societies give us permission to show. The intensity of grief can feel 'unnatural', due to societal expectations, and the pursuit of a return to 'normal life' as soon as possible. Caution should be exercised against pathologising grief, unless there is a genuine medical or mental health concern.

Despite precursors that may lead to complicated grief, not everyone affected by these factors will develop it. With adequate support, and sufficient resilience, many people adapt to their losses over time, without intervention. A significant number also experience post-traumatic growth after complicated grief, with or without any professional support (Calhoun and Tedeschi 2010).

As we have explored, definitions of complicated grief can be arbitrary. It can also be confused with depression, anxiety, post-traumatic stress disorder (PTSD), and any other physical, or psychological disorder. According to the DSM-5 and the proposed ICD-11, PGD and PCBD are separate grief-related conditions, but they can exhibit similar, or the same symptoms, as other disorders such as depression.

Colin Murray Parkes (1980, p.6) states, 'We should not assume that every bereaved person will need counselling.' However, in the case of a diagnosis, or for those at high risk of developing complicated grief, specialised treatment has been proven effective (Shear 2015).

As mentioned at the beginning of this chapter, professionals are not in agreement over what constitutes complicated grief, and many believe its inclusion in the DSM-5 pathologises what is a natural experience. Feminist psychologist Leeat Granek is one such academic who believes that labelling grief as a disorder distorts the notion that grief is normal and creates cultural norms that are deviant (Granek 2013). She, and others, believe that these challenges after a loss can be the response to an unsupportive cultural environment, and to expectations of the bereaved, rather than signifying a medical condition.

The death of a child

Many people have concrete dreams and ideas of what their children, and life as parents, will be like, even before conceiving a child. This can begin unconsciously, or consciously, at a very young age, particularly in children who mimic parental roles. For many people, 'when I grow up and have children' is ingrained within the psyche, it is a cultural norm, or an assumption.

Therefore, the relationship a parent has with their child may have started within their imagination many years prior to conception. This is the only relationship that is physically, internally created, all other relationships are external. Children are the combination of the parents' DNA, ego and future dreams. When a child dies, it is common to hear parents speak of wanting to follow their child, to be near them, and be physically present with them. *There is a physical part of them that also died.*

The child does not have to have independent life for grief to arise. Bereavement can also occur following a miscarriage, ectopic pregnancy, stillbirth, therapeutic termination and abortion.

Therese Rando (1986) has observed there are experiences parents may share after the death of a child, these include:

- a shattered assumptive world

- anger due to the unnatural order of child death (which can also occur with a miscarriage, ectopic pregnancy, stillbirth or infant death, as well as the death of an adult child)

- guilt from a perception of failure to protect their child

- a diminished sense of self with a questioning of 'Who am I?' (e.g. with a full-time mother, the death of an only child can challenge her primary identity).

Rando describes many other losses, due to the projections of future hopes and dreams, and the roles that the child played within the family. For example, with perinatal deaths there is an empty nursery, or it could be the loss of a first grandchild. If the child was an only child, there can be the perception of a loss of identity as a parent. Answering the difficult question of 'Do you have children?' can be challenging.

One misconception that endures is that the divorce rate for bereaved parents is always higher than in the general population. Research conducted by Rando argues against this. Educator and researcher Reiko Schwab (1998) has also provided research to support the view that relationships can survive the death of a child, and may even be strengthened in the long term. This is known as post-traumatic growth.

The death of a baby, either in gestation, during birth or shortly after birth, can sometimes be perceived as less significant than a child death. However, the significance of the loss can be determined by the attachment, and dream projection, and for some people, these deaths have the same impact. For example, research by Gold *et al.* (2016) on the occurrence of depression and PTSD in mothers after a perinatal death found that they had a fourfold increased risk of depressive symptoms and a sevenfold increased risk of developing PTSD. There is an expectation that a pregnancy will result in the birth of a healthy child, with all the dreams associated with that child and its future development. When perinatal death occurs, this assumptive world is shattered.

As with any death, meaning making and continuing bonds are significant to bereaved parents, whatever the age of the child.

You are arranging a funeral with an older man who has recently lost his wife to cancer. The death was anticipated after a long illness, but he appears overly distraught and confused. Is he suffering from complicated grief?

There is only one way to find out if he is suffering from a form of complicated grief, and that is through an assessment by a specialist. He could potentially have complicated grief from a previous bereavement, due to his wife's illness, the death may have been traumatic, or he may simply be an intuitive griever.

Does miscarriage have the same bereavement impact as the death of an adult child?

It depends on the person involved. For some parents, a miscarriage can be an event that they accept and process without difficulty, for others it is as devastating as a child's death. For some parents, particularly those who have challenged fertility (either difficulty conceiving or with a history of multiple miscarriages), the attachment may have been formed prior to the pregnancy. In their imagination, the child, and the future of the child, has already been constructed, imagined and psychologically lived.

Chapter 5

HOW DO YOU SUPPORT THE BEREAVED?

Grief can be debilitating, and the impact of a significant bereavement should not be underestimated. For this reason, grievers may need support, and providing the space and time for them to speak or act, without fear of being judged, can be invaluable to them. The opportunity to talk about their loved one, and the sharing of memories, may be avoided by friends and family for fear of 'upsetting' them, but the bereaved are already 'upset'.

The griever's expectation gap

Grievers may be uncertain about what they need, or want, and may struggle to express themselves. The expectation gap is where grievers do not express themselves in a way that is easily understood. It is also used to demonstrate where the bereaved may be unable to communicate at all. In each case, it is difficult for others to interpret the communication, or lack of communication; this is demonstrated in Figure 5.1. Friends and family generally want to support grievers, but they may not be aware the griever has expectations of them.

If grievers do not communicate their needs, family and friends may assume the griever is fine, or conversely, they may feel they are not wanted. This may result in them feeling rejected or ignored which can lead to further misunderstandings.

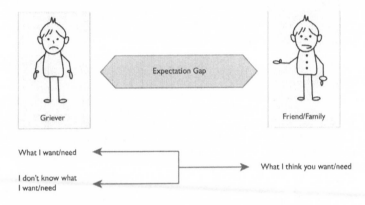

Figure 5.1: The griever's expectation gap (Rustam Eltman)

Just as emotional support can sometimes be neglected due to misunderstandings, practical support may also be overlooked. There are many practical ways to help: cooking, cleaning, dog walking, assisting with funeral arrangements, completing paperwork, babysitting, and driving are some examples. Instrumental grievers may particularly value task-based support, whereas intuitive grievers may prefer emotional support. Whilst different types of support should not be viewed as exclusive to either grieving style, it may be helpful to consider what the griever's needs are.

Emotional support

Providing emotional support includes spending undetermined time with someone, actively listening to them, helping them, advising them if appropriate, perhaps alongside helping in practical ways such as cooking or driving for them. These are all designed to support, and provide feelings of wellbeing to help someone cope with the life changes they are dealing with. Emotional support is what the bereaved may need, for as long as they need it, in whatever form is most helpful to them.

Offering sincere empathy and compassion to someone who is grieving, allowing them to express how they are feeling, can be considered 'holding a space' for them. It is allowing them to express their emotions, including crying, or being silent. It is allowing them to reminisce about the deceased without interrupting. It is allowing them to communicate how they are feeling, what they are thinking, what they are experiencing, what decisions they are making, without hijacking their stories with yours. It is about being neutral and caring, and allowing them to express themselves. Offering emotional support means the focus is on the bereaved, not the person providing support. Even if you have suffered a similar bereavement, you do not know how that person is feeling, because you are not them.

However, not everyone wants to talk about their feelings or share their thoughts, and they should not be pressured into doing so. Intuitive and/or extrovert grievers may welcome the opportunity to express their emotions, but instrumental and/or introvert grievers may not. As we learnt earlier, this does not mean they are not grieving 'properly', or doing it 'wrong'.

By contrast, counselling overlays emotional support with a theoretical structure. It is designed to facilitate a process of change within a boundaried supportive environment. Research suggests that most bereaved people do not need such a facilitative process. C.M. Parkes says, 'We should not assume that every bereaved person will need counselling' (Parkes 1980). However, a therapeutic environment may be helpful if the griever does not have a sufficient support network, or is unable to ask friends or family for support. Support from a bereavement professional may also be helpful for impartial support. Many bereavement charities offer support services, or can signpost to the most suitable organisation. There is a list of reputable organisations towards the end of this book, but this is not exhaustive.

Supporting the bereaved parent

Bereaved mother Kelly set up a blog, Chasing Dragonflies, following the death of her daughter Abi. She recommends a five-step approach to a bereaved parent entitled 'STALL', which means: Smile, Talk, Approach, Look and Listen. This framework is simple but very necessary, due to our awkwardness with a parent whose child has died, as it can be difficult to find the right approach. STALL can be summarised as:

Smile: Smile warmly, say hello and pause to talk for a moment if you feel it's appropriate.

Talk: On your very first encounter with a bereaved parent you should try to talk to them. In fact, you should try to talk to them as soon after the event as possible.

Approach: There are no words you can say that will help make this terrible tragedy any easier for the bereaved mum, and plenty you can say that won't, so the best thing I think to do is to approach her and give a gentle touch on the arm or a quick squeeze of the hand. Bereaved mums can feel like little lost lambs, so having someone to simply sit or stand with them can really help.

Look: Eye contact is everything – it's words, hugs, tears all rolled together – so look the mum in the eye, but avoid looking overly sympathetic.

Listen: Just listen...don't be afraid of the tears of grief. Don't feel you should fill the void with platitudes. Just pause. Be quiet, add a few comforting words and take the cue from them. It will help them more than you know.

Kelly has kindly allowed us to reproduce her blog here, and whilst she is writing from the perspective of a bereaved mother, for other mothers, her principles can be applied to any bereavement.

It is helpful to ask open questions when communicating with the bereaved. For example, asking 'How are you feeling?' rather than 'Are you feeling better today?' Open questions allow someone to express themselves openly, whereas closed questions invite a 'Yes' or 'No' answer. When the griever is answering open questions, listen to them attentively, without distractions if possible. To build trust and support someone, that person needs to feel heard, and that they are in an environment where they are respected.

Grief is an intensely personal experience. One mother whose son died states, 'I hate it when people *hijack* my grief. They didn't know him, so don't send me text messages on his birthday, that's *my* day to grieve, not your day to inflict yourself on me' (Dyson, personal communication, 2017). Every parent is different and some will appreciate messages but others will not. If the parent is openly talking about their deceased child, they may appreciate the support, but those who do not talk to you about their child may want you to respect their privacy.

Bereaved children and young people

Children know more than they are often given credit for; they are also more resilient than might be appreciated. It is usually the adults that are uncomfortable talking about death, dying and bereavement. Adults may avoid talking openly with, or in front of, children to protect them, but children don't need death 'hidden' from them. This may be because the adults are uncomfortable or are not sure what to say.

There are three overriding factors to consider with bereaved children:

- If the parent is coping, the child will generally follow.

- Children grieve at their life stage, and re-grieve as they grow older, as their understanding of life grows.

- Children and young people can grieve just as deeply as adults, but their understanding of it depends on their cognitive and emotional maturity.

Despite grief being unique, we can generalise about what death looks like, and the possible reactions to it, depending on the child's age. Research findings recommend that children receive support from their parents, friends and their school or nursery (Harrington and Harrison 1999).

The interaction of child development and reactions to grief, can be generalised into three stages:

1. *Pre-school*: These children are usually too young to understand what death or dying means, although they will be aware that someone is missing. They will also be conscious of any physical and emotional changes around them. Their reactions may involve deviations from their normal patterns of eating, sleeping and/or crying. There may also be a heightened anxiety surrounding separations or regressive behaviour.

2. *School age*: The older children are, the more they understand that death is finite. They also become aware that death can happen to anyone, and this may lead to a preoccupation with death. They may exhibit attention-seeking behaviour or experience nightmares. They will ask questions appropriate to their cognitive ability. Their ability to cope will improve with age and experience. Their schoolwork and peer relationships may be affected.

3. *Adolescence*: Young adults have the cognitive ability to understand death, dying and bereavement as concepts, but they do not have the adult experience to contextualise them. Their coping mechanisms are still in development. Peer support is critical for

adolescents, who may be adversely affected by the other psychological and physical changes at this life stage. They may become withdrawn, or respond with more risk-taking behaviour. They may also exhibit anger or sarcasm. This is a particularly difficult stage of life, so bereavement can be very difficult to deal with. School involvement is important, because bereaved adolescents can be singled out as 'different', which can lead to bullying.

School is a significant part of a child's life and should be involved in supporting the emotional needs of grieving children. Aoife M. Lynam, a teacher and expert in children's grief, states that 'children are coming to school with more than just the bags on their back' (Lynam, personal communication, 2017). An integrated approach involving the parents, peers and teachers should be encouraged.

Children can exhibit changes in their behaviour following a bereavement. These are some examples of the signs to look out for if there are variations from their normal behaviour:

- anxiousness or nervousness

- selfishness or narcissism

- confusion or less focus than normal

- anger or guilt regarding the death

- pessimism or excessive worry.

The list is endless, but any change in normal behaviour may have a root in the bereavement and may be an expression of grief. As adults' behaviour changes in response to the emotions of the loss of the person, children can be affected in similar ways, but they may not be able to express this verbally. Changes in behaviour are not ordinarily a cause for concern unless they do not abate or are overly severe. Children will also react to their parents' emotions and actions, so it's always advisable to support the parent first because usually this creates a chain reaction resulting in the improvement of the child's behaviour.

Children do not have the life experience of adults, so may not have the tools to equip themselves for coping with these life changes. It is always best to be open and to interact with them in an age-appropriate way. Death is a natural part of life, and acknowledging this fact contributes to their education and healthy emotional development.

An example of teaching children resilience after a bereavement, whilst supporting them appropriately, is demonstrated at Good Grief, an organisation in New Jersey, who provide children with a room to paint whatever they choose. Allowing children to express themselves freely encourages engagement. This allows the adults to understand what the child is feeling and provide the most suitable support to facilitate coping mechanisms, thus building resilience. This room is now almost completely covered in graffiti. There are many other age-appropriate ways to allow children to express themselves creatively. These can include children's bereavement workbooks, grief books or any other suitable medium.

When we observe children, they demonstrate normal grief, prior to the imposition of cultural expectations. It is natural for them to talk to and about the deceased and dream about them.

Rituals and continuing bonds are important for children too

Children find it natural to ask questions within a safe and trusted environment, and this should not be discouraged. After 30 years of teaching about death and bereavement in US schools, Stevenson (2004) reported that those receiving death education had reduced fear of change and loss, enjoyed better communication with their families, and had performed better than expected in other subjects. But whilst children can be open within a trusted environment, they tend to be reluctant to be open within school due to the desire to fit in (Holland 2008).

The children and grandchildren of a deceased person are the most enduring, tangible, physical example of continuing bonds. It is surely logical to include them, in an age-appropriate way, in conversations, memorialisation, and anything else that refers to the deceased person. *They are, quite simply, the deceased person's legacy.*

Compassion fatigue

To support someone else, particularly someone in a vulnerable position, the supporter should ideally be emotionally stable. However, self-care is often not prioritised by the caregiver or the environment they are working within. It can be difficult to look after someone else if you aren't looking after yourself. Within the caring professions there is an expression that their job is like gas: it takes up as much space as you allow. Boundaries are integral to self-care.

One of the dangers for caregivers in any capacity, whether paid or unpaid, is compassion fatigue:

> Compassion fatigue has been described as the 'cost of caring' for others in emotional and physical pain. […] It is characterized by deep physical and emotional exhaustion and a pronounced change in the helper's ability to feel empathy for their patients, their loved ones, and their co-workers. It is marked by increased cynicism at work, a loss of enjoyment of our career, and eventually can transform into depression, secondary traumatic stress, and stress-related illnesses. The most insidious aspect of compassion fatigue is that it attacks the very core of what brought us into this work: our empathy and compassion for others. […] Compassion fatigue is an occupational hazard, which means that almost everyone who cares about their patients/clients will eventually develop a certain amount of it, to varying degrees of severity. (Figley 1995)

In his book *Man's Search for Meaning*, Viktor Frankl includes clear examples of compassion fatigue: where, surrounded by death in a concentration camp, it ceases to have an impact. Whilst an extreme example, it serves to demonstrate how this can be applied to any scenario where death occurs daily or in numbers.

Being aware of the signs of compassion fatigue, and taking steps to mitigate it, are all within the scope of self-care. Typical signs that may be experienced include:

- exhaustion: emotional, physical, and/or psychological

- stress and/or anxiety

- feelings of failure or apathy.

Professionals should be aware that you *can't anchor a drifting boat to an unsecured buoy*. Having a supervisor or confidante you can speak to about your experiences, without compromising the identity of the bereaved, is very important.

Cumulative grief

Compassion fatigue is the result of stress and the subsequent apathy towards caring for someone with emotional needs. Whilst there may be a sharing of common symptoms, cumulative grief is different. It is the repeated experience of death, and the impact of grief multiple times, without sufficient time to process each individual occurrence. This can feel overwhelming. Compassion fatigue and cumulative grief often have similar impacts, which can include avoidance, detachment, stress and feelings of helplessness.

Cumulative grief is prevalent in medical staff, particularly those working in end-of-life care, oncology and paediatrics, but can occur with any professional who is regularly exposed to death:

> When pediatric oncology fellows at two academic centers were interviewed about their experiences with the deaths of their patients, they endorsed feelings of sadness, guilt, failure, and helplessness. Fellows also expressed feeling vulnerable, inexperienced, unable to cope, and alone in their reactions to death, and they attributed their negative experiences to inadequate modeling of coping strategies, lack of grief counseling and other supportive resources, and extensive ward duties that exhausted their physical and emotional reserves. Not every oncologist suffers from extreme grief, yet many do experience at least some degree of these feelings at some point in their careers, suggesting the importance of making room for such emotions in our clinical practice. (Kaye 2015)

Kaye indicates there two key areas to consider:

- *Awareness*: Cumulative losses for both professionals and individual grievers require special consideration and support.

- *Support*: Medical professionals require support; their feelings and experiences require understanding and validation.

Emotional and physical exhaustion, whether resulting from a professional role, or while supporting a griever, can be overwhelming. As a society, and within organisations, we should be promoting a culture of awareness, understanding and support. Anyone experiencing compassion fatigue or cumulative grief should be able to seek and obtain support.

Creating or maintaining boundaries can be difficult for some, but it is important to protect the bereaved, as well as the carer. As the griever may be in a vulnerable position, it is easy for them to become dependent on someone who is showing them empathy and giving their time freely. It is the professional's responsibility to manage the relationship and ensure they are supporting the bereaved in a compassionate way, whilst ensuring the bereaved person is not becoming dependent on the professional's time, or believing that the professional is their friend.

There is a difference between befriending and engaging in a friendship. The former is where the relationship is concentrated on the person being supported; the focus is entirely on them, not the befriender. The latter is sharing thoughts, experiences and stories in a two-way exchange.

Charlotte was five years old when her elder sister died. Her parents decided she should not attend the funeral because it would upset her. Her parents also never talked about death, or her sister in front of her. What are your thoughts on this scenario?

Babies and toddlers are obviously too young to express themselves, so parental decisions are made until a child is able. Children should be consulted about their wishes regarding whether they should attend a funeral, or other related events. As children re-grieve when their knowledge and cognitive ability develops, if a child feels they were excluded, they may feel disenfranchised.

Children may want to be included in conversations about the deceased, and it is healthy for them to be included in continuing bonds. Engaging them with age-appropriate playing, writing, drawing or specific grief workbooks for children may help facilitate the conversation and allow free expression.

What should schools do when a pupil is bereaved?

First, there should be a bereavement policy that is a living document. A recommended resource for schools introducing, revising or reviewing their bereavement policy or procedures is *Responding to Loss and Bereavement in Schools* by John Holland (2016). All policies should include a plan of action to support on a school level, for the individual pupil and the teachers involved in the child's welfare.

Second, the policy should be followed in practice. If the policy has been well considered, the needs of the pupil within the school environment should be supported, and the staff will be prepared. There are various ways to ensure implementation is appropriate and timely, Dyregrov suggests the following:

- Let handling of death in the school or classroom setting be the theme for a teachers' meeting.

- Organise or send teachers and/or other staff members… to a course on children and death.

- Select a smaller group of teachers…to increase their knowledge in this area, so that they can be a resource group for the other staff.

- Make sure that the school or kindergarten has relevant literature that can be used by interested staff, and material/literature and web addresses that can be used in the classroom or playgroup.

- In response to an event, quickly establish the involved people, what has happened, how it happened and what information has been given out.

(Dyregrov 2008, pp.125–126)

Third, the teachers involved with the pupil should also be supported. Teachers and pupils are both part of a wider environment that involves not only legal obligations, but welfare considerations too. Peer support is critical to older children, but they may not have the tools to support a bereaved friend. A supportive educational environment can help facilitate this process in a manageable way.

If a pupil or teacher dies, this may affect the whole school. The bereavement policy should have guidelines on how to facilitate this situation.

Research by educator and researcher Aoife M. Lynam at Trinity College, Dublin found that children were reluctant to talk about death, dying and bereavement in school. Schools should be mindful that children require support in understanding the changes that are happening in their life, but they may be unable to express this in a school environment (Lynam, personal communication, 2017).

CONCLUSION

Always remember: It is not your story, it is their story.

Whilst there are plenty of resources to support the bereaved from an intuitive perspective, this book was written to provide a basic understanding of grief from both intuitive and instrumental perspectives. It is intended for anyone supporting the bereaved in any capacity, and instrumental grievers. Many frontline professional staff: teachers, nurses, funeral directors, social workers, counsellors and celebrants have inadequate or no training in up-to-date bereavement theory, and this book seeks to redress that.

It should be clear that every bereavement, whether experienced by an adult or child, is unique, and most are normal and natural expressions of the loss of a significant attachment. Grievers generally want empathy and support in a way that is suitable for them whilst they are mourning. In rare cases, grief can be complicated and may require specialised treatment. But in all cases, any support or intervention provided needs to consider the uniqueness of that person and the relationship they had with the deceased.

Everyone has a story, and the bereaved may welcome the opportunity to tell theirs.

The story of loss created with chalk on a pavement in Dublin, 2016

There is no uniform, prescriptive approach to grief; no 'right' things to say, no 'right' things to do because everyone is different. What is acceptable to one person may not be to the next; what should be encouraged is authenticity. It is recommended to employ sensitivity, empathy and genuineness. It is always better to say, 'I'm sorry, I don't know what to say' than to say nothing at all. The bereaved person may potentially be experiencing the most devastating event in their life, this demands respect and consideration of their vulnerability at a time that they may need support the most.

Silence does not require filling, and crying should not be discouraged.

The role of resilience after a bereavement may be under-recognised and has a significant impact on grieving outcomes. Many people discover they are more resilient than they may have thought prior to the death and resume a different, but 'normal', life afterwards.

It seems fitting to end with a quote from Colin Murray Parkes OBE, psychiatrist and well-known author on grief, with one of his visions for the future:

> …where parents as well as children, leaders as well as followers, receive the cherishing and support that they need; where the griefs that are a necessary part of life are recognised as such and those who suffer them receive understanding and wise counsel. (Parkes 2002, p.383)

FURTHER RESOURCES

This list is not exhaustive; it is intended to provide an overview of online resources and organisations that can be contacted for further information. Bereavement charities and support organisations are aware of others who support in this area, so can signpost to additional resources. If you are searching for something specific that is not listed, an online search may yield results, but caution should be exercised that the information provided is reputable and supported by professionals. The recommended alternative is to contact a general bereavement organisation such as Cruse Bereavement Care, the Irish Hospice Foundation or a similar organisation that will be able to help.

Bereaved children

The Childhood Bereavement Network

www.childhoodbereavementnetwork.org.uk

The Childhood Bereavement Network (CBN) is the hub for those working with bereaved children, young people and their families across the UK. They underpin their members' work with essential support and representation, bringing them together across localities, disciplines and sectors to improve bereavement care for children.

National Alliance for Grieving Children

www.childrengrieve.org

The National Alliance for Grieving Children provides resources, grants and support for grieving children across the US. Online resources are extensive and they also provide up-to-date signposting information.

Family Lives On Foundation

www.familyliveson.org

Family Lives On Foundation supports the lifelong emotional wellbeing of children whose mother or father has died. Their Tradition Program provides opportunities for intentional remembering, creating a haven for grief, communication and celebration.

Good Grief

www.good-grief.org

Good Grief have extensive online resources for anyone supporting bereaved children.

Grief Encounter

www.griefencounter.org.uk

Their vision is that every bereaved child in the UK, and their family, receives access to high-quality professional support to help alleviate the emotional pain caused by the death of a loved one.

Irish Childhood Bereavement Network

www.childhoodbereavement.ie

Online resources and training for parents, carers and professionals supporting bereaved children.

The Moyer Foundation

www.moyerfoundation.org

The mission of The Moyer Foundation is to provide comfort, hope and healing to children and families affected by grief and addiction. Its innovative resources and programmes address the critical needs of children experiencing powerful, overwhelming and often confusing emotions associated with the death of someone close to them or substance abuse in their family.

Winston's Wish

www.winstonswish.org

Winston's Wish provides professional support, a helpline, and resources and publications to support bereaved children. They are a specialist provider of support for children bereaved through homicide and suicide.

Bereaved military families

SAAFA

www.ssafa.org.uk

SAAFA is a military charity in the UK, which supports bereaved families when a loved one was serving in one of the armed forces. They offer support and signposting to other specific military bereavement resources.

TAPS

www.taps.org

TAPS support anyone who is grieving the death of someone who died whilst serving in the US military. It has a support line, 'survival kits', counselling services, online support, befrienders, events and signposting.

Bereaved through alcohol and drugs

The Bead Project

www.beadproject.org.uk

The Bead Project is a joint partnership between Cruse Bereavement Care and Adfam to specifically support those bereaved through alcohol and/or drugs.

Bereaved through homicide

Parents of Murdered Children

www.pomc.com

A membership organisation to support those parents bereaved through homicide and the professionals who support them. There is online signposting and it is supported by many legal professionals. There are chapters in many US states.

SAMM

www.samm.org.uk

A charity providing support to the bereaved and professionals following the bereavement by murder or manslaughter.

Bereaved young people

Hope Again

www.hopeagain.org.uk

Hope Again is Cruse Bereavement Care's website for young people. Cruse is a national charity that provides support, advice and information to children, young people and adults when someone close to them dies.

Bereavement after road fatality

Brake

www.brake.org.uk

RoadPeace

www.roadpeace.org

Both Brake and RoadPeace have helplines and support literature to provide emotional support, practical information and signposting for the bereaved after a road fatality. They both offer helpline callers referrals to face-to-face support or other appropriate tailored support, along with advice for professionals such as police Family Liaison Officers, teachers and others caring for road crash victims. They also both have a tribute webpage dedicated to the memory of those who have died in road crashes.

European Federation of Road Traffic Victims

www.fevr.org / www.WorldDayofRemembrance.org

FEVR is a global campaigning organisation that created the World Day of Remembrance for the bereaved.

Irish Road Victims Association

www.irva.ie

IRVA provides free information and support to the bereaved after road accidents.

Bereavement by suicide

Centre for Suicide Research

http://cebmh.warne.ox.ac.uk/csr/research.html

The Centre for Suicide Research at the University of Oxford has links to other organisations for bereavement after suicide both within the UK and globally.

Living Links

www.livinglinks.ie

Living Links provides outreach, practical help, advice and support to those bereaved by suicide.

Support after Suicide

www.supportaftersuicide.org.uk

This website has extensive links to resources for supporting someone after a suicide in the UK. It has information for the bereaved and professionals including information on forms, the police and coroners.

Survivors of Bereavement by Suicide

http://uk-sobs.org.uk

Support after bereavement by suicide can be found on this extensive website for the bereaved, professionals and carers. There are extensive online resources, local support groups, a helpline, e-support, retreats and a wealth of further information.

Child death

Bereaved Parents

www.bereavedparentsusa.org

Bereaved Parents of the USA was founded by a group of bereaved parents from across the country to offer support, understanding, encouragement and hope to fellow bereaved parents, siblings and grandparents after the death of a child.

Charlies Angel Centre

www.charlies-angel-centre.org.uk

This charity provides telephone and email support to any parent that has suffered the death of a child. Their campaign has an online memorial, holds events and provides information and support.

Child Bereavement UK

www.childbereavementuk.org

Child Bereavement UK supports families and educates professionals when a baby or child of any age dies or is dying, or when a child is facing bereavement.

Compassionate Friends

www.compassionatefriends.org

The Compassionate Friends is an organisation that consists exclusively of bereaved parents supporting other bereaved parents. The US website has links to all chapters across the world and an online support forum for bereaved parents.

Complicated grief

The Center for Complicated Grief

www.complicatedgrief.columbia.edu

Provides resources, workshops and training for professionals.

Digital legacy

Digital Legacy Association

www.digitallegacyassociation.org

This UK-based organisation has extensive online resources including toolkits, leaflets and reports for the public and professionals. It also provides training on issues around digital assets and digital legacies.

General bereavement

Bereavement Ireland

www.bereavementireland.com

A registered charity providing counselling and online resources to the bereaved in Ireland.

Cruse

www.cruse.org.uk

An extensive online resource with information for grievers and professionals, including training events and specialist projects. The helpline has a directory with every support organisation in the UK and Northern Ireland. Each Cruse branch also has a directory of all local support organisations within their catchment area.

Grief Directory

www.griefdirectory.org

Extensive online resources and a directory for grief support: websites, products, resources, etc. in the US.

Grief Journey

www.griefjourney.com

Dr Bill Webster has online podcasts for the bereaved and professionals and is particularly helpful for intuitive grievers.

The Irish Hospice Foundation

www.hospicefoundation.ie

The Irish Hospice Foundation has online videos and audio recordings for the bereaved and professionals. They have an extensive training programme, library and online resources.

Leeds Bereavement Forum

www.lbforum.org.uk

Leeds Bereavement Forum has an extensive and updated list of bereavement-related website links across the UK in its 'Directory of Services'.

What's Your Grief

www.whatsyourgrief.com

This site is particularly useful for online support for instrumental grievers. They also have theory-based blogs for professionals looking to expand their knowledge in bereavement. The website is an extensive resource for the bereaved and professionals alike.

Miscarriage, stillbirth and neonatal death

The Miscarriage Association

www.miscarriageassociation.org.uk

The Miscarriage Association offers online support and information to anyone affected by the loss of a baby in pregnancy. They have a helpline, raise awareness of miscarriage, and offer resources to professionals.

Pregnancy Loss Directory

www.pregnancylossdirectory.com

An international site signposting to miscarriage, stillbirth and baby-loss support organisations.

Sands

www.sands.org.uk

Sands supports anyone who has been affected by the death of a baby before, during or shortly after birth. The have a helpline for parents, families, carers and health professionals; a UK-wide network of support groups with trained befrienders; an online forum and message boards enabling bereaved families to connect with others; and a wide range of leaflets, books and other resources available online and in print.

SiMBA

www.simbacharity.org.uk

SiMBA is a Scottish charity that offers online resources for baby death, miscarriage and stillbirths.

Spouse/partner death

Modern Widows Club

www.modernwidowsclub.com

This is a US-based organisation that holds events, provides support and has an informative blog.

Widowed and Young

www.widowedandyoung.org.uk

This is a UK-based organisation that has a lot of useful resources on its website for young widows and widowers. It also includes resources on what to say to widows and widowers and how to help them practically.

Widow.ie

www.widow.ie

Widow.ie is a moderated online forum for widowed men and women to interact with each other.

Sudden death

Sudden

www.suddendeath.org

Sudden is a charitable initiative supporting people bereaved suddenly by any cause. They have extensive online resources and signposting and provide training and webinars for grievers and professionals.

Twin death

Lone Twin Network

www.lonetwinnetwork.org.uk

The Lone Twin Network is a voluntary support group run by and for lone twins, over the age of 18. Whilst they are UK based, they have many members worldwide.

TAMBA

www.tamba.org.uk

The Tamba Bereavement Support Group (BSG) exists to support all parents and carers of multiples who have experienced loss whether it was during pregnancy, at birth or at any point afterwards. They offer parent-to-parent befriending and an online Facebook group support.

REFERENCES

Ainsworth, M.D.S. (1973) 'The Development of Infant–Mother Attachment.' In B. Cardwell and H. Ricciuti (eds) *Review of Child Development Research* (Vol. 3, pp.1–94) Chicago, IL: University of Chicago Press.

American Psychiatric Association (2013) *Diagnostic and Statistical Manual of Mental Disorders* (5th edn). Arlington, VA: American Psychiatric Publishing.

Ariès, P. (1991) *The Hour of Our Death.* New York, NY: Oxford University Press.

Bassett, D.J. (2015) 'Who wants to live forever? Living, dying and grieving in our digital society.' *Social Sciences, 4,* 4, 1127–1139.

Bonanno, G.A. (2004) 'Loss, Trauma, and Human Resilience: Have We Underestimated the Human Capacity to Thrive After Extremely Aversive Events?' *American Psychologist, 59,* 1, 20-28. Accessed 20 October 2017 at http://dx.doi.org/10.1037/0003-066X.59.1.20.

Bowlby, J. (1969) *Attachment. Attachment and Loss: Vol. 1. Loss.* New York, NY: Basic Books.

Brennen, B. and Hardt, H. (1999) *Picturing the Past: Media, History and Photography.* Urbana: University of Illinois Press.

Bronfenbrenner, U. and Morris, P.A. (2007). 'The Bioecological Model of Human Development.' In W. Damon and R.M. Lerner (eds) *Handbook of Child Psychology: Vol. 1. Theoretical Models of Human Development.* Hoboken, NJ: John Wiley & Sons.

Calhoun, L.G. and Tedeschi, R.G. (2010) 'Posttraumatic Growth.' *The Corsini Encyclopedia of Psychology.* doi:10.1002/9780470479216.corpsy0698.

Carey, I.M., Shah, S.M., DeWilde, S., Harris, T., Victor, C.R. and Cook, D.G. (2014) 'Increased risk of acute cardiovascular events after partner bereavement: A matched cohort study. *JAMA Internal Medicine 174,* 4, 598–605.

Delaney, S. (2016, 23 July) 'Grief: It's complicated (10% of the time).' Irish Association of Humanistic and Integrative Psychotherapy [Blog post]. Accessed on 20 July 2017 at http://iahip.org/inside-out/issue-77-spring-2016/grief-its-complicated-10-of-the-time.

Doka, K.J. and Martin, T.L. (2010) *Grieving Beyond Gender: Understanding the Ways Men and Women Mourn.* New York, NY: Brunner-Routledge.

Dreher, D. (2013, 18 May) 'Grief and the DSM-5.' *Psychology Today* [Blog post]. Accessed 20 July 2017 at www.psychologytoday.com/blog/your-personal-renaissance/201305/grief-and-the-dsm-5.

Dyregrov, A. (2008) *Grief in Children: A Handbook for Adults.* London: Jessica Kingsley Publishers.

Figley, C.R. (ed.) (1995) *Compassion Fatigue: Coping with Secondary Traumatic Stress Disorder in Those Who Treat the Traumatized.* New York, NY: Brunner/Mazel.

Freud, S. (2005) *On Murder, Mourning and Melancholia.* London: Penguin Books.

Global Ecology Network (2011) 'World birth and death rates.' Accessed on 8 July 2017 at www.ecology.com/birth-death-rates.

Gold, K.J., Leon, I., Boggs, M.E. and Sen, A. (2016) 'Depression and posttraumatic stress symptoms after perinatal loss in a population-based sample.' *Journal of Women's Health, 25,* 3, 263–269.

Granek, L. (2013) 'Disciplinary wounds: Has grief Become the identified patient for a field gone awry?' *Journal of Loss and Trauma 18,* 3, 275–288.

Gupta, D.S. (2015, 10 March) 'How grief can make you sick.' Everyday Health [Blog post]. Accessed 20 July 2017 at www.everydayhealth.com/news/how-grief-can-make-you-sick.

Harrington, R. and Harrison, L. (1999) 'Unproven assumptions about the impact of bereavement on children.' *Journal of the Royal Society of Medicine, 92,* 230–232.

Hazan, C. and Shaver, P. (1987) 'Romantic love conceptualized as an attachment process.' *Journal of Personality and Social Psychology, 52,* 3, 511–524.

Holland, J. (2008) 'How schools can support children who experience loss and death.' *British Journal of Guidance & Counselling, 36,* 4, 411–424, DOI: 10.1080/03069880802364569.

Holland, J. (2016) *Responding to Loss and Bereavement in Schools: A Training Resource to Assess, Evaluate and Improve the School Response.* London: Jessica Kingsley Publishers.

Kaye, E.C. (2015) 'Pieces of grief.' *Journal of Clinical Oncology, 33,* 26, 2923–2924.

Kilcrease, W. (2008, April 20) 'Stages of grief – time for a new model.' Accessed on 14 August 2017 at https://www.psychologytoday.com/blog/the-journey-ahead/200804/stages-grihttps://www.psychologytoday.com/blog/the-journey-ahead/200804/stages-grief-time-new-modelef-time-new-model.

Klass, D., Silverman, P.R. and Nickman, S.L. (eds) (1996) *Continuing Bonds: New Understandings of Grief.* New York, NY: Routledge.

Kübler-Ross, E. (1969) *On Death and Dying.* New York, NY: Macmillan.

Lindemann, E. (1944) 'Symptomatology and management of acute grief.' *American Journal of Psychiatry, 101,* 2, 141–148.

Maciejewski, P.K., Maercker, A., Boelen, P.A. and Prigerson, H.G. (2016) '"Prolonged grief disorder" and "persistent complex bereavement disorder", but not "complicated grief", are one and the same diagnostic entity: An analysis of data from the Yale Bereavement Study.' *World Psychiatry, 15,* 266–275.

Morrow, W.C. and Cucuel, E. (2013) *Bohemian Paris of to-day.* Rockville, MD: Wildside Press.

Mostofsky, E., Maclure, M., Sherwood, J.B., Tofler, G.H., Muller, J.E. and Mittleman, M.A. (2012) 'Risk of acute myocardial infarction after the death of a significant person in one's life: The determinants of myocardial infarction onset study.' *Circulation 125,* 3, 491–496.

Neimeyer, R.A. (2000) 'Searching for the meaning of meaning: Grief therapy and the process of reconstruction.' *Death Studies 24,* 6, 541–558.

Neimeyer, R.A. and Sands, D.C. (2011) 'Meaning Reconstruction in Bereavement: From Principles to Practice.' In Neimeyer, R.A., Harris, D.L., Winokuer, H.R. and Thornton, G.F. (eds) *Grief and Bereavement in Contemporary Society:Bridging Research and Practice* (pp. 9–22). New York: Routledge.

Newberg, A.B. and Waldman, M.R. (2013) *Words Can Change Your Brain: 12 Conversation Strategies to Build Trust, Resolve Conflict, and Increase Intimacy.* New York, NY: Plume.

Nowinski, J. (2012, 21 March) 'When does grief become depression?' *Psychology Today* [Blog post]. Accessed 20 July 2017 at www.psychologytoday.com/blog/the-new-grief/201203/when-does-grief-become-depression.

Oliveira, A.J., Rostila, M., Saarela, J. and Lopes, C.S. (2014) 'The influence of bereavement on body mass index: Results from a national Swedish survey.' *PLoS ONE 9,* 4. doi:10.1371/journal.pone.0095201.

Parkes, C.M. (1988) 'Bereavement as a psychosocial transition: Processes of adaptation to change.' *Journal of Social Issues, 3,* 53–65.

Parkes, C. M. (1980) 'Bereavement counselling: does it work?' *British Medical Journal, 281,* 6232, 3–6.

Parkes, C. M. (2002) 'Grief: Lessons from the past, visions for the future.' *Death Studies, 26,* 367–385.

Parkes, C.M. (2014) 'Diagnostic criteria for complications of bereavement in the DSM-5.' *Bereavement Care, 33*, 3, 113–117.

Petch, A. (n.d.) Funeral and mourning clothing. Accessed on 14 August 2017 at http://web.prm.ox.ac.uk/england/englishness-funeral-clothing.html.

Prigerson, H.G., Horowitz, M.J., Jacobs, S.C., Parkes, C.M. *et al.* (2009) Prolonged grief disorder: Psychometric validation of criteria proposed for DSM-V and ICD-11. *PLoS Medicine 6*, 8. doi:10.1371/journal.pmed.1000121.

Rando, T.A. (1986) *Parental Loss of a Child*. Champaign, IL: Research Press.

Roazen, P. (1992) *Helene Deutsch: A Psychoanalyst's Life*. New Brunswick, NJ: Transaction.

Schut, H.A.W., Stroebe, M.S., van den Bout, J. and Terheggen, M. (2001) 'The Efficacy of Bereavement Interventions: Determining Who Benefits.' In M. Stroebe, R. Hansson, W. Stroebe and H. Schut (eds) *Handbook of Bereavement Research: Consequences, Coping, and Care* (pp.705–737) Washington, DC: American Psychological Association.

Schwab, R. (1998) 'A child's death and divorce: Dispelling the myth.' *Death Studies 22*, 5, 445–468.

Shear, M.K. (2006) 'The treatment of complicated grief.' *Grief Matters: The Australian Journal of Grief and Bereavement 9*, 2, 39–42.

Shear, M.K. (2015) 'Complicated Grief Treatment (CGT) for Prolonged Grief Disorder.' In U. Schnyder and M. Cloitre (eds) *Evidence Based Treatments for Trauma-Related Psychological Disorders* (pp.299–314).

Shermer, M. (2008, November 01) 'Five fallacies of grief: Debunking psychological stages.' Accessed on 14 August 2017 at https://www.scientificamerican.com/article/five-fallacies-of-grief/.

Stevenson, R.G. (2004) 'Where do we come from? Where do we go from here? Thirty years of death education in schools.' *Illness, Crisis and Loss 12*, 231–238.

Stroebe M.S. and Schut H. (1999) 'The Dual Process Model of coping with bereavement: Rationale and description.' *Death Studies 23*, 197–224.

Stroebe, M., Stroebe, W., Schut, H. and Boerner, K. (2017) 'Grief is not a disease but bereavement merits medical awareness.' *The Lancet 389*, 10067, 347–349.

Tonkin, L. (2008) *Coping with the Impossible, In Our Own Words: Parents Talk About Life After Their Child Has Died of Cancer*. London: CLIC Sargent UK.

Volkan, V.D. (1981) *Linking Objects and Linking Phenomena: A Study of the Forms, Symptoms, Metapsychology, and Therapy of Complicated Mourning*. New York: International Universities Press.

Worden, J.W. (2010) *Grief Counselling and Grief Therapy: A Handbook for the Mental Health Practitioner*. London: Routledge.

INDEX